The Rhodesian SAS
At War

Andy Ryan

The copyright to this book is owned by the author. All rights reserved. No part of this publication may be reproduced, stored in a retrieval system, or transmitted in any form, electronic, photocopying, mechanical, recording or otherwise, without prior permission from the author.

This Book Uses UK Spelling
And Imperial measurements

Other books by Andy Ryan on the same theme
which you may be interested in.

Bravo Ten

The Rhodesian SAS: Their Greatest Missions

**Combat & Survival Secrets of the Rhodesian
SAS**

More books by the same author are also available
in eBook and paperback formats
From Amazon or selected booksellers.
Please search Bravo Ten Andy Ryan for a full
list.

Foreword

This book introduces the reader to some of the Rhodesian SAS operations which were conducted throughout the duration on the Bush War. It is by no means an exhaustive list, as to cover all SAS missions would require many volumes. Its aim is to give a taste of the involvement of the SAS throughout that conflict by detailing specific instances across the Bush War timeline and the impact C Squadron 22SAS (later 1stRSAS) had on the communist terrorist enemies of Rhodesia.

If you would like to read about the SAS mission to kill ZIPRA leader Joshua Nkomo in Lusaka, Zambia; the attack on the oil storage depot in Beira. Mozambique; the stunning daylight assault on the ZIPRA intelligence service HQ in Lusaka; and the beyond top secret plan to re-take control of Zimbabwe Rhodesia from Robert Mugabe, as well as other operations, then please see my other book 'The Rhodesian SAS: Their Greatest Missions'.

Andy Ryan.

One: Beginnings. 1966

I presume your interest in Rhodesia is enough to already have the necessary knowledge surrounding political events which led to UDI and the subsequent bush war, therefore I'm not going to go over 'old ground' in any great detail. Aside from giving an overview of the three leading political personalities in this section, the book concentrates on SAS operations. There is only reference to the 'bigger picture' to give context to some of the missions described herein.

The Rhodesian SAS (or C Squadron 22SAS as it was then known) had lain virtually dormant since its return from Malaya. C Squadron had been raised to assist British efforts against the communist terrorist threat in that country and had quickly proved itself a vital cog in the SAS machine. *For your information, because the Rhodesian Squadron was part of the British regiment is the reason why there is no C Squadron in today's 22nd SAS.*

By the time Rhodesia made her unilateral declaration of independence (UDI), C Squadron was little more than a Platoon sized outfit, however, the Rhodesian military's decision to retain a Special Forces capability was to prove fortuitous when the opening shots of what was to prove the fiercest conflict in sub-Saharan Africa were fired.

African nationalism was sweeping the continent inspired, in part, by the British 'winds of change' philosophy. The political movements known as ZANU (Zimbabwe African National Union) and ZAPU (Zimbabwe African People's Union) emerged from this time and were quickly transformed from politically impotent 'irritants' into what the Rhodesian government regarded as serious threats to national security. Both groups fostered military wings; ZANLA (Zimbabwe National Liberation Army) and ZIPRA (Zimbabwe People's Revolutionary Army) for ZANU and ZAPU respectively. Both were fully aligned to communist doctrines and supported by the USSR and China – with China backing ZANU.

Ian Smith was born in 1919, to British parents who had settled in Southern Rhodesia. He attended boarding school and, afterwards, Rhodes University College, in South Africa. At the outbreak of the Second World War, Smith was eager to join the fight. At this time he was still at university and his ambition to volunteer for the Royal Air Force was frustrated by an edict by the Southern Rhodesian government, which forbade university students from joining the military until after they'd graduated. Undeterred, Smith managed to sidestep the restriction.

After his entry onto the Empire Air Training Scheme he trained as a pilot, graduating in 1942. Subsequently, Smith flew Hurricane fighters in the Middle-East. A crash saw him seriously injured and he was not deemed fit to fly again until 1944. While piloting a Spitfire over Italy, Smith was shot down by flak. He evaded capture and eventually joined a partisan group, fighting alongside them for several months until eventually making his way back to allied lines.

Back in Rhodesia, after the war, Smith entered politics, becoming an MP aged 29 (the youngest MP in Southern Rhodesian history).

Throughout the 1950's and 1960's, when Britain was busying itself with decolonization, political options available to Southern Rhodesia via the existing parties seemed limited to Smith and his colleagues. As a result he was instrumental in founding The Rhodesian Front, principally in a bid to counter the threat he saw looming from 'the winds of change'. This eventually led to the Unilateral Declaration of Independence on November 11th 1965.

Robert Mugabe was the leader of ZANU. He'd been born in the then Southern Rhodesia in 1924. Despite his poor upbringing, Mugabe was college educated and worked as a teacher in Southern and Northern Rhodesia as well as Ghana. His long held anger at minority white rule led him into politics, where he embraced Marxism. His political activities in Southern Rhodesia soon brought him to the attention of the authorities and he was eventually imprisoned after being found guilty of sedition. Upon his release he fled to Mozambique, where he established himself as leader of ZANU and ZANLA and thereafter directed operations against Rhodesia for the duration of the bush war.

Joshua Nkomo was born in 1917. After primary school, Nkomo completed a yearlong carpentry course at industrial school before finding work as a driver. He later returned to carpentry, teaching the subject. He went to live in South Africa and while there met Nelson Mandela and other future nationalists. Upon his return to Southern Rhodesia, Nkomo became involved in the trade union movement, eventually rising to lead the Black Railway Workers Union and the Rhodesian branch of the African National Congress (ANC).

Nkomo was eventually jailed and, after his release, went to Zambia where he determined to carry on the struggle against the white Rhodesian regime.

***

Only a matter of months after declaring UDI, Rhodesia found herself subjected to the first recorded terrorist infiltrations of the conflict. In one instance a heavily armed group of ZANLA crossed the border from neighbouring Zambia to mount a programme of attacks against various targets. Once inside Rhodesia, the gang split into two sections. The first group struck out for Umtali with orders to destroy the oil pipeline which ran from Beira, Mozambique, to Umtali and disrupt the area's electricity supplies by sabotaging power lines.

With the Rhodesian Police (BSAP) Special Branch alerted to the fact that terrorists were at large within the interior of the country, a large-scale operation to round them up was mounted. This particular mission entailed both regular police and reservists and was successful insofar as the Umtali bound group was intercepted near Sinoia before they could cause any damage or loss of life. The terrorists put up fierce resistance when they found themselves cornered and attacked by the BSAP (British South African Police) and Rhodesian Air Force ground attack aircraft, but were overpowered and taken prisoner after losing several men killed.

The second group managed escaped the attention of the BSAP and just three weeks later, that same group was responsible for an incident which many Rhodesian's regarded as the start of the bush war.
At Nevada Farm, a remote homestead about fifteen miles from Hartley, a group of ZIPRA terrorists attacked and killed Johannes Viljoen and his wife Barbara. The only 'witnesses' to the crime was the couple's two young children, three-year-old Tommy and his nine-month-old sister Yolanda (who only survived by virtue of the fact they were both asleep in bed).
Both Johannes and Barbara had not only been shot dead in their own home, but those responsible had gone on to mutilate their bodies. It was a terrorist crime which outraged Rhodesia. Something had to be done to bring the culprits to justice.

The BSAP pulled out all the stops in their effort to hunt down the Viljoen's killers. In May 1966 'Operation Pagoda' was launched to track down and kill or capture the terrorists responsible. The police, supported by troops from No.1 Commando Rhodesian Light Infantry, took to the bush in pursuit.

***

The shockwaves from the Viljoen murders reverberated around Rhodesia and were felt throughout the High Command of the Rhodesian Security Forces (RSF). An order was duly issued to the SAS to take retaliatory action against ZANU.

At that point in time C Squadron was less than fifty men strong. As such its offensive capability was restricted to small unit actions. As there were only a few officers, it was also effectively administered by its senior NCOs and it was to the SNCOs that the baton was passed.

The SAS wanted to hit ZANU hard and make it known that attacks on Rhodesian civilians would result in counter strikes which would cause the terrorists grievous harm. A list of possible targets was considered until it was decided that the most effective way to hit the enemy would be to destroy the epicentre of terrorist operations; ZAPU headquarters. Everyone involved at that stage knew that this would be a far from easy task. ZANU HQ was situated in the suburbs of Lusaka, the capital of Zambia. The reason why it was chosen was not only the fact that its destruction would be a significant blow in terms of morale to the ZANU machine, but it housed thousands of carefully collated ZANU records; if they could be wiped out the terrorist machine would grind to a halt for an indeterminate period of time.

Attacking a target in the middle of a capital city in a neighbouring country with the extremely limited resources at the raiding party's disposal would take considerable lateral thinking. A straightforward attack in the conventional sense was out of the question; for a start it wasn't needed, but to go in 'noisy' would generate a response from the Zambian police and military (the latter of whom were quartered in the vicinity of the target). Any contact with the local forces would mean fighting in the streets of the Zambian capital – a country that Rhodesia wasn't at war with. That would cause all manner of diplomatic issues and serious repercussions for Rhodesia among the international community. Given the fact that there were only a few men available for the task meant that guile would have to be at the forefront of the operation throughout its various phases.

It was decided that the best method of destroying the ZANU HQ would be by the use of high explosives. Intelligence reports furnished by CIO (Central Intelligence Organisation – the Rhodesian equivalent of the CIA or MI6) indicated that the ZANU HQ wasn't guarded during the periods it was unoccupied, so a team of saboteurs could break in under cover of darkness without fear of compromise and plant specially constructed explosive charges at a strategic points within the building where their detonation would most likely cause structural failure and collapse. To 'implode' the target building would considerably lessen the chances of collateral damage to surrounding properties while still ensuring the mission would be completed.

It was agreed that utmost secrecy would surround the operation and, as such, only a handful of senior officers were made aware of what was in the offing.
The raiding party itself was made up of four SAS men, led by none other than the CO of C Squadron himself; the deeply experienced and highly respected Major Coventry.

I'll divert slightly for a short period to explain a little about Major Coventry, as his own history gives the reader an understanding of the calibre of men serving with C Squadron at that time.
Born and raised in the UK, he was commissioned as a

Second Lieutenant in the East Lancashire Regiment in 1938. He later volunteered to fight in the Finnish 'Winter War' against the invading Soviet army. Upon his return to the UK he applied to join the newly formed commandos. After completion of training he joined No5 Commando. Later wartime service was with 'Special Raiding Forces Middle East' (a composite group of commando, Special Boat Service, Greek Sacred Squadron and Long Range Desert Group). In 1944 he transferred to 45 Royal Marines Commando and stayed with that unit until after the war. Thereafter he joined the Parachute Regiment and went on to serve in Malaya where he was attached to C Squadron SAS. After emigrating to Southern Rhodesia, Major Coventry joined the Rhodesian Light Infantry and from there – perhaps inevitably – became CO of C Squadron 22SAS.

Major Coventry had chosen C Squadron's SSM to act as second in command. The callsign also included one man who wasn't a regiment member; the person in question was a senior officer of the BSAP who'd been seconded for the task. Why would a police officer find himself involved in a military operation, let alone an SAS mission which would take him into another country to carry out an act of sabotage? The answer to that lies in the fact that the increasing violence was officially classed as an insurgency, with responsibility for the Rhodesian response falling to the civil power. Just as what happened in Northern Ireland during the troubles, at that time the military were brought in to aid the civil power as and where required.

The group was assembled and began an exhaustive period of rehearsal; at this point none of them (save for the callsign commander, Major Coventry) knew the details of the mission.

The plan was to cross the Zambezi River into Zambia using collapsible 'Klepper' canoes and, after hiding the boats, the party was to make their way to a rendezvous point where a vehicle driven by a Rhodesian undercover agent operating in Zambia would transport them to Lusaka and the target. After the explosive charge was laid, the team would retrace their steps, returning to the boats and Rhodesia.

It was straightforward plan, which all good plans are, and gave the raiding party the best chance of success. They'd be on the ground in Zambia for the minimum possible time and the planners were confident that their men would be able to escape the attentions of the Zambian authorities by virtue of the fact that the demolition charge was to be initiated by time fuse, meaning that the SAS would be gone from Lusaka and well on their way back to the Zambezi before any explosion.

With rehearsals complete and the final go ahead for the operation issued, the team were ferried by truck to the vicinity of the jumping off point. Security considerations and the lay of the land meant that the final leg of the journey to the southern bank of the Zambezi had to be made on foot. After arriving close to the water's edge, but while remaining well in cover, the team began their final preparations. The demolition charge was laid among the equipment as the team began the task of assembling the Klepper's. Suddenly there was an almighty explosion, the pressure wave from which carried a long way through the bush and across the water. Somehow, the charge had prematurely detonated, catching all those within the vicinity. Several of the men were killed instantly with the rest mortally wounded. The only man to survive was the callsign commander, Major Coventry. Although wounded, his life had been saved by virtue of the fact he had bent down to tie his bootlace a second or so before the explosion and was shielded from the full force of it by a fold in the ground in which he'd inadvertently placed between himself and the others.

Given the security surrounding the mission, there were no other units in the area who could offer assistance. The only point of contact between the callsign and the outside world was a BSAP post a couple of miles downriver. An RLI detachment which was stationed at the police post to carry out anti-terrorist patrols along the border heard the explosion and was intrigued; as far as they were concerned there were no friendly forces in the area so the explosion could only be the work of ZIPRA terrorists. There was nothing to demolish in that sector so the blast presented a conundrum; perhaps a terrorist gang, inbound from Zambia had suffered some kind of accidental or negligent discharge of explosives they were carrying?

While the police contacted their regional HQ to pass on details of the incident, the Sergeant Major in charge of the RLI detachment got a party of men together and set off into the bush to investigate.

It wasn't long after that the commandos came across Major Coventry as he made his way towards the police post in search of help. Unflappable to the end, the Major greeted the Sergeant Major (who he knew from his own days with the RLI), giving no hint that he'd just survived death by a whisker. After filling in the warrant officer on the bare bones of the story, the Major and the RLI returned to the police post where the officer's wounds could be attended to (both Major Coventry's eardrums had been perforated in the blast) and another RLI group dispatched to recover the bodies of the deceased then bring them to the police post.

The following morning a helicopter arrived to transport Major Coventry and the bodies of his men to Salisbury. After silently watching the loading of his dead troops, the Major climbed aboard the helicopter as it prepared for takeoff. As it climbed into the morning sky, the aircraft suffered a mechanical failure which sent it plunging the 100 feet back to earth. It was only due to the skill of the pilot that both he and Major Coventry walked away unscathed and the chopper suffered only minor crash damage. Unruffled by yet another near death experience, Major Coventry stepped out of the chopper as the police and RLI men ran up to help and was heard to coolly quip 'I wonder what will happen next?'

What should have been the SAS's first external operation of the war had ended in disaster. They had not even made it out of Rhodesian territory before four of the Squadron's best and most senior operators were killed. The BSAP had also lost a high ranking officer.

Questions were asked about what may have caused the explosive device to prematurely detonate. Normally, the SAS would make up their own charges, but this one had been fabricated in Salisbury and had a built in detonation mechanism. No one would ever know the precise cause, but it was presumed that the detonator had somehow primed itself during its journey by truck. However careful a driver tried to be, it was inevitable that the bomb would be bounced around as the truck negotiated the rough tracks leading towards the Zambezi.

It was a most unfortunate start to C Squadron's war.

***

The disaster which had overtaken C Squadron's first 'external' could never be enough to derail other plans. Soon the SAS were planning another operation. The target was the same – ZANUs Lusaka HQ. With one eye on what happened when the making up of an explosive device was 'outsourced' the SAS were determined to make sure that they would be responsible for every facet of this mission.

This time, instead of using high powered plastic explosives to shatter the building and cause its collapse, the forthcoming mission would see it burned to the ground. The most efficient way of achieving this was by the use of incendiaries. The compound of choice when the SAS wanted to destroy by fire was thermite. Thermite is a mixture of metal oxide and metal powder (usually aluminium). When ignited, it burns with great intensity, producing very high temperatures in a short space of time; as a result it quickly causes devastating fire. The SAS team would break in to the ZANU HQ under cover of darkness and lay several thermite charges. They would be timed to detonate after the SAS had left the scene, thus allowing them to make good their escape.

While that phase of the operation more or less mirrored the aborted one, the makeup of the callsign involved and method of delivery was drastically different.

In all, three SAS men – Lieutenant Brian Robinson and two Sergeants – were selected to carry out the job. The infiltration into Zambia would not be made by canoe but aeroplane. The planners decided that the callsign were to be flown in a light aircraft to a bush airstrip south of Lusaka. The flight would be made at low level and with navigation and landing lights switched off. Simply finding what was, in effect, a needle in a haystack was a challenge in itself; there were no fancy navigation aids available to aircraft of that type in those days, but landing in the dark without lights was the greatest challenge of all. Fortunately, the Rhodesian's had a pool of highly experienced pilots who were skilled enough to carry out such high risk manoeuvres. In order to lessen the chances of something going wrong, the mission would only be launched when the weather conditions were correct and the moonlight was enough to provide an acceptable degree of visibility.

Once on the ground the SAS were to be met by a CIO agent whose job was to transport them to Lusaka and the vicinity of the target then back again.

Preparations began in earnest. The infiltration phase was fraught with danger and no one took the prospect of landing a light aircraft in the dark on a bumpy bush airstrip lightly. After what had happened to Major Coventry's party, C Squadron could ill afford to lose any more men, so it was imperative that the pilot selected to fly the callsign into Zambia was able to practice. A couple of weeks prior to the launching of the mission, he flew his plane out to the Bulawayo area where he was able to rehearse without fear of being seen by locals or interrupted by terrorists.

A disused bush landing strip was selected for the pilot's use as it resembled the one he'd be flying the team into on the night and, fortunately but also by design, it was roughly the same distance from the FAF (Forward Airfield) he'd been sent to as the target field in Zambia. The personnel manning the FAF weren't aware of the reason why the light aircraft was carrying out night-time manoeuvres and they knew better than to ask.

Flying in the dark with no navigational aids then landing with no lights and only the moonlight to see by proved every bit as challenging as it would first appear, but the skill and experience of the pilot meant he was able to successfully rise to the challenge.

Meanwhile, back in Salisbury, the three SAS men assigned to the task of destroying the ZANU Headquarters were making their own preparations.

The target building lay in close proximity to others, some of which would be occupied at the time the attack was scheduled to take place, therefore it was imperative that entry to the ZANU HQ was carried out quietly and unseen. Although there were no guards present and no security alarm system in place (such things were virtually unheard of beyond places like banks) the building was kept locked when empty. The SAS team attempted various techniques to refine a method of forcing entry into the building, most of which produced far too much noise, before settling on one which could be relied on to work.

For Lieutenant Robinson and the others, a point of great

concern was the fact that they had no clear intelligence about the ZANU HQ so were unable to determine small details which could stop them in their tracks. For example, were the doors and windows barred? If they were then there'd be no breaking in. If that proved to be the case, their only hope of success would be to smash a window and – after hastily re-rigging the charges which had been made up 'ring main' fashion – dropping a thermite bomb inside in the hope it would have the desired effect before the fire brigade turned up.

For this job the callsign would wear civilian clothes and, as the operation was 'deniable', all trace of Rhodesian origin would be removed. No documents of any kind were to be carried and – aside from the CIO man who would take them back to the airstrip after the job – no provision for help or rescue made. The callsign didn't even have a radio, so if they found themselves in trouble then they'd have no alternative but to make their escape as best they could. That would mean an overland trek on foot through the bush towards Rhodesia while a lot of angry Zambian troops gave chase. As the crow flew they'd face a journey of almost sixty miles (not that they'd be able to march on a single bearing) before having to find some way of crossing the Zambezi River back into friendly territory.

Planning and rehearsals over, it was time to go….

The Callsign emplaned and took to the skies. The pilot kept his plane at low level all the way so as to avoid the search and tracking radars which formed part of Lusaka's southern air defence network. With that in mind, the landing site could not be too close to Lusaka as, even with at low altitude, the risk of being spotted increased the closer the aircraft got to the city.

Despite all the difficulties, the pilot managed to find the airstrip without problem, throttling the engine back to cut the noise as he made his final descent. The shallow gliding approach was followed by a neatly executed landing and the little Cessna rolled along to the far end of the strip. Eager to be gone, the SAS callsign was out of the plane as soon as it stopped rolling and disappeared into the cover of the surrounding bush. The aircraft turned and made to take off; so far so good.

As they listened to the receding aero engine, Lieutenant Robinson and the two NCOs struck out in search of their CIO contact. They knew he was waiting to meet them at the end of the runway but, after a brief search it suddenly dawned on them that they didn't know which end of the runway! After double checking that they hadn't missed him in the darkness, the trio trudged the full length of the strip in the hope that the CIO man was waiting there.

Following anther search they finally happened upon the agent. After satisfying each other as to their identities by swapping passwords, the CIO man led the callsign to his car (which had been fitted with false Zambian number plates especially for the task). During their briefing the SAS team had been told that Zambian police and military presence was virtually nonexistent through the area they were to travel, so the chances of coming into contact with any patrols or roadblocks were negligible. However, that proved to be another nugget of information that was shot down in flames when the agent announced that the local police had been out and about of late to conduct random stops on passing vehicles. The team quickly conferred to produce an 'actions on' plan in the event that they were compromised by Zambian police. Although they were all armed, there would be no shooting; killing civilian Zambian police wouldn't be looked upon favourably by anyone. If they could not bluff their way through a stop they'd simply have to abort the mission, remove themselves from the scene as quickly as possible then make their way back to the airstrip to await the arrival of the Cessna.

As luck would have it the roads were deserted and after

an uneventful forty mile journey from the airstrip they made it to Lusaka.

Lusaka was (and still is) a vibrant modern city and as they passed through its brightly lit suburbs, the SAS men were becoming increasingly confident that the plan was going to work. The CIO agent explained that he would drive past the target building to give Lieutenant Robinson and the others a chance to see it before dropping them off around the corner. Incredibly, the SAS men had only seen a few photographs of the ZANU HQ, and these weren't even supplied by Rhodesian intelligence, but came courtesy of a magazine article which had been written about the place a few months earlier!

As the car drove along the street the scene the men inside was confronted with staggered them all into silence. The place was thronging with youths who were engaged in a full-scale street brawl. As the CIO man picked his way through the fighting Lieutenant Robinson and his men stared out at the ZANU headquarters. Instead of being cloaked in darkness, the lights were on inside the building; someone was at home! Whether or not there were ZANU officials working late, or a security guard or two (who they'd been promised wouldn't be there) none of them knew but, as a couple of lights actually went on and off as they passed, it was clear that the place was occupied.

Clearing the immediate area, the CIO man brought his car to a halt in a quiet side street. What now? It was clear that every scrap of information they had was faulty. Instead of a deserted street there were countless rampaging youths and – most important of all – the promise of finding an empty target building had gone up in smoke. After a quick conflab, the SAS men decided that they could possibly salvage something from the wreckage of all their misleading intelligence reports. They'd leave the car then skirt around the area, avoiding the fighting and probable police reaction and then approach the ZANU HQ from the rear, where a patch of open waste ground would afford them some cover. Perhaps, just perhaps, the noise and confusion of what was happening on the street could be used to the SAS men's advantage, allowing them plant one or more of the thermite bombs where they'd do most damage. It was possible there might be an open window in an unoccupied room where one of the thermite bombs could be 'posted' or, perhaps, the noise from the fighting might prove such that it could cover the team as they broke a window? If the SAS were to plant a device in this way, they'd have to adapt it beforehand; paring back the fuse accordingly so the thermite would detonate seconds after the fuse was pulled. As for those inside the building, well they'd just have to run for it when they began to smell burning. The confusion of it all and the difficulty the fire brigade would have in responding to the blaze amid the chaos playing itself out on the street would also help the SAS. If the fire was seen by the occupants, even after the thermite charge had only just initiated, there was simply no way they could extinguish it. It would simply be too violent and spread too quickly for that to happen (as anyone reading this who has experience of handling thermite can attest to).

The callsign made it to the waste ground without incident. Here in the darkness beyond the overspill of the streetlights, they settled down to take a look at the rear of the building. It was immediately apparent that the immediate area surrounding the target was lit so well that there was virtually no chance of making an unseen approach; it would have been dangerous enough had the place been empty, but the chances of sudden compromise by those inside or the battling street gangs was simply too great. Figures could be seen bobbing in and out of view at one upstairs window; it would take one quick glance – perhaps prompted by something in the peripheral vision – for the occupants to see three white men approaching across the back lawn.

Could they simply wait awhile in the hope that the disorder would peter out and those inside the ZANU HQ would go home? It was now approaching midnight and there was no indication of the fighting stopping anytime soon. The Cessna was due to collect them at 0200 so, Lieutenant Robinson concluded, there was simply not enough time left to carry on.

The team returned to the car and the waiting CIO man. With the mission scrubbed there was nothing else to do for the agent but drop his passengers off at the place where they were to rendezvous with the aircraft. The SAS had planned to be lifted to safety not from the bush airstrip but none other than Lusaka International Airport.

With Zambian radar operators always on the alert for possible breaches of their airspace from Rhodesian planes, it was a risky undertaking, but the planners thought it perfectly workable just so long as the plane went in at very low level. While the focus on the infiltration was not to be seen, the aircraft being picked up on radar during the exfiltration phase was not as much of an issue. After evading the radar defences and ignoring the air traffic controllers as it made its approach, all the little Cessna had to do was land (on the grass if necessary) then quickly taxi to the appointed place where the SAS would be waiting to be taken aboard. A quick turnaround then takeoff would ensure the Rhodesian's would be gone before anyone knew what was happening and the airport police could intervene. It would then be a case of low flying all the way home. With confusion in their favour, the team would arrive back in Rhodesia before the Zambian's knew what had happened. It was a bold plan but, as the saying goes; 'Who Dares Wins'.

The SAS callsign was deposited on the outskirts of the airport. They approached and entered by scaling the perimeter fence at a point on the edge of the field which was far enough away from normal airport activity to be seen. After quickly finding the rendezvous point, they settled down to wait.

0200 hours came and went with no sign of the Cessna. As the minutes ticked by the SAS men were becoming increasingly anxious. Had there been some technical hitch which meant the Cessna couldn't take off? The Rhodesian's had a spare aircraft on standby for such an eventuality so, that being the case, the subsequent delay would be only minimal. If the aircraft had crashed on route (which was a distinct possibility given the conditions under which it was operating) then there would be no plan B. The callsign knew they couldn't wait indefinitely so would have to have their own cut off point, after which it would be presumed the plane would not be coming to get them. Any move to remove themselves from the precincts of the airport must be carried out before dawn if they were to stand a chance of evading the attention of airport workers and clear the area.

Even during this known slack period of airport activity there were still enough routine flights to get the hopes of the hidden SAS men up. More than once they heard what they thought to be a light aircraft only to realise it was some other propeller driven machine.

At about 0230 Lieutenant Robinson and his men saw a Cessna rolling towards them. They had been watching every part of the field upon which they thought the plane would come but were surprised to see the little plane follow a Zambian Airways aircraft as it came in to land on one of the main runways. Quickly, the SAS team flashed the recognition signal and, in acknowledgement the plane was brought to a halt. Breaking cover, the SAS men sprinted for the Cessna and clambered aboard. The Pilot brought the aircraft round in a 180 degree turn before opening up the throttle. After a short takeoff run, the plane left the ground, staying low as it turned for home.

Back in Rhodesia the questions came thick and fast. It was imperative that lessons were learned from the failure of the operation so that they wouldn't be repeated in the future. During the debrief the SAS team were quizzed about the details of the mission and what exactly had gone wrong. It was clear from the start that the SAS had placed far too much reliance on faulty or incomplete intelligence. Using a magazine as the primary source of their understanding of the workings of the ZANU headquarters was something straight out of a stage farce.

Nothing could be done about the street fighting, as that was beyond anyone's control, but the fact that the raiding party was assured that the target was unoccupied and unguarded was unforgivable as it was later learned that it was attributed to some snippet of hearsay. It wasn't only the terrible information with which the team had been furnished which came under the spotlight, but aspects of the planning. That small but vitally important slip up which led to the SAS (and the CIO agent) not knowing which end of the bush airstrip to rendezvous at could have cost the operation before it even got started. Had the SAS team not managed to find the CIO man, they'd have been well and truly marooned behind the lines. Given the time constraints involved there was no way they could have walked to Lusaka Airport to be picked up, instead they'd have been trekking south while hoping for the best.

For C Squadron, lessons had to be learned from the operation. Everyone knew that while this incursion into Zambia was the first time the SAS had set foot outside Rhodesia in this increasingly violent conflict, it most definitely wouldn't be the last.

TWO: INTO MOZAMBIQUE. 1969

Despite their overall ineffectiveness up until that point in the conflict, incursions by terrorists from Zambia continued to pose problems for the under-resourced Rhodesian police and military authorities, but what was happening in the east soon became a grave cause for concern. Mozambique had been under Portuguese control for many years. Now, with a growing and increasingly violent counterinsurgency campaign being fought against their forces across the country, as well as political instability at home, the Portuguese military were finding it difficult to maintain order.

Ranged against the Portuguese was FRELIMO (the Front for the Liberation of Mozambique). FRELIMO had grown from a few dissenting voices into a well organised guerrilla movement which dedicated itself to the forcible removal of Portuguese rule and establishment of its own government. FRELIMO had proved itself a serious threat to the Portuguese rulers, scoring considerable successes against the 'occupying' army.

Rhodesian observers knew that the Portuguese hadn't the heart for a fight to the death. Their troops were mainly conscripts who had little or no interest in this far-flung African colony, let alone a desire to defend it. If the Portuguese were to abandon Mozambique, FRELIMO would take control. Their anti-Rhodesian sentiment was clear, even at that stage, so it was feared that the country would soon become home to ZIPRA and ZANLA, effectively opening up a second front along the vulnerable almost 900 mile long border. There were other strategic considerations, such as access to Mozambique's Indian Ocean ports would be cut off, severely restricting trade between landlocked Rhodesia and the rest of the world (at that point in time sanctions had yet to be fully implemented).

As far as the Rhodesian government was concerned, it was vital that the Portuguese remain in control.

It was a request from the Portuguese military authorities which eventually found its way into SAS hands. The previous year, 1968, FRELIMO had begun a concerted effort to wrest control of the Tete province from the colonial power. It was a campaign which had borne much fruit for FRELIMO. The Portuguese quickly found themselves under enormous pressure, with the result that they had ceded much ground to their opponents. Instead of getting out into the bush to take on FRELIMO head to head, the Portuguese military had made the critical strategic mistake of withdrawing to various strongpoints where it remained, sedentary and useless, while the enemy was allowed the run of the countryside.

When the request finally landed on the desks at SAS HQ in Salisbury (which, at that time, was a corner of Cranborne Barracks; the home of the Rhodesian Light Infantry) it was clear that that it was top secret in nature.

The Rhodesian government did not want it to be known that its forces were operating in Mozambique. Given the constraints in manpower which was always of concern to C Squadron, its commitments to terrorist incursions from Zambia, and the need to stay firmly under the radar, it was quickly decided that the best and most effective course of action would be to insert a couple of four-man callsigns into Tete. Once on the ground, each team's task would be to find the locations of FRELIMO camps then call in airstrikes by Portuguese Air Force (PoAF) planes. The SAS knew that – if done correctly – devastating losses could be wrought upon FRELIMO for minimal expenditure of effort from the Portuguese; certainly enough to take FRELIMO off the front foot throughout the region.

Working from Portuguese military intelligence reports, the SAS realised that most of the main FRELIMO bases were located in the north of the province, close to the Zambian and Malawi borders, so it was here that their efforts would be concentrated. The area to be searched was large, very large, but thorough map appreciations and estimations of likely locations were made so as to narrow the odds.

The two teams were selected and began their preparations. The first deployment would be three weeks in duration and the mission itself would be undertaken on foot. A lot of equipment was needed to sustain the men over that period and Bergen packs became monstrously heavy as a result.

Once out in the bush, and in order for the SAS callsigns to maintain an effective communications link with the Portuguese, a specialist team of radio operators from the Rhodesian Corps of Signals were to be dispatched to the main Portuguese military base in Tete. These men, from 10 Signals Squadron, were often used in support of the SAS and their expertise ensured that messages could be relayed over the long distances and often challenging atmospheric/ground conditions involved between SAS callsigns and home.

When the preparations were complete, the SAS/Sigs teams were flown to Mozambique then on to Tete province. The following day, both SAS callsigns were inserted into the start points of their respective patrol areas courtesy of PoAF Alouette III helicopters (of the same type used by the Rhodesian Air Force).

It wasn't long before both teams started to find spoor which indicated movements of large bodies of men (the SAS trackers were so experienced as to be able to pick out many vital clues among tracks). The details were duly noted down and passed back to the 10 Squadron team during their scheduled radio transmissions. Apart from relaying messages back to Rhodesia, the SAS liaison officer who was working alongside the signallers would pass the information to the local representatives of Portuguese military intelligence, CISMIL (Centro de Informacoes e Segurance Militares) who would then, in turn, inform the relevant commanders. At that point in time both the SAS and Rhodesian planners shared the belief that all credible intelligence being passed on to the Portuguese military would be acted upon. Action by ground troops to disrupt these lines of communications would have hampered the FRELIMO operations which were having such a detrimental effect upon the Portuguese in the region.

After a week or so of searching, one of the SAS callsigns happened upon a large FRELIMO base. They'd used the directions taken by the spoor they'd encountered to pinpoint the possible location of such a facility and homed in on it accordingly. The camp was large, housing at least five hundred FRELIMO (or Freddie as they were known to the Rhodesian's).

After setting up a covert observation post where they could observe the routines of the camp, it became clear that it was being used as a Forward Operating Base from which FRELIMO forces were being deployed to attack the Portuguese within one particular area of the Tete province. A detailed map of the area was compiled along with a full description of the patterns under which it operated; the latter, along with map coordinates and salient topographical features with which to pinpoint it and the approaches to it from the air, were passed back to 10 Squadron's signallers. The SAS callsign then settled down to wait. They were confident that they'd soon be informed that the PoAF were to mount an airstrike on the camp, after all, this is what the Portuguese had asked the Rhodesian's to get involved for. Hitting this target would prove a real victory for the Portuguese and a terrible blow for FRELIMO and – if followed up with other such attacks on enemy facilities as and when they were identified – would quickly turn the tide of events in the

Portuguese favour.

When it came, the 'airstrike' left the onlooking SAS team speechless. The PoAF had been instructed that the best time to hit the target was during its morning parade, when FRELIMO were gathered in several large groups across the centre of the camp. One pass, using 500 or 1000 lb high explosive bombs would decimate the camp's residents before they knew what was happening. Follow-ups could then concentrate on those who survived as well as the camp itself, flattening it and everything in it.

The following day a pair of FIAT G-91R fighter bombers of the PoAF came screaming in to make a low pass over the camp. Morning parade had been and gone and the inhabitants dispersed to the four corners of the target. Incredibly, both machines failed to drop any of their ordnance, passing away into the distance before turning to make another run. This second pass was equally perplexing as, again both aircraft simply flew over the camp before disappearing back to base.

The SAS callsign reported the details of the incident and were told to stay in position until further notice. By now they could see that the camp was being evacuated, FRELIMO had been well and truly alerted to the fact that their camp had been discovered and were in no mood to hang around and wait for the PoAF to return.

The following day, the Portuguese were back. This time they dropped their bombs but it was far too late, the camp was empty. The opportunity to kill or incapacitate several hundred of the enemy had been thrown away. As far as the SAS was concerned it was sheer madness!

That first covert SAS operation into Mozambique ended in frustration for the Rhodesian's. Subsequent missions – all run on the same top secret basis – were to prove equally exasperating. Despite having countless targets located for them, the Portuguese army proved most reluctant to capitalise on the advantages being handed to them by the SAS. They seemed genuinely fearful of leaving their own strongholds to get to grips with the enemy. In an environment where small unit action was the order of the day, the Portuguese would only ever deploy in large numbers, giving FRELIMO ample opportunity to escape before they could be engaged. Later, when SAS tracking teams were being attached to provide eyes and ears for Portuguese ground units, they would often point out the presence of FRELIMO in the vicinity to find that the Portuguese would simply ignore them, stopping to drink from the crates of beer they had brought along while the enemy made good their escape! Sometimes they were known to make as much noise as possible while deploying – even banging mess tins together – in order to 'scare off' nearby FRELIMO before they could get into a contact!

For the unmotivated Portuguese conscript soldier, there seemed little value in dying for a cause he neither believed in nor understood.

For C Squadron bosses and the Rhodesian military hierarchy in general, the die had already been cast: the reports of Portuguese military's unwillingness and inability to control the ever expanding FRELIMO threat meant it was only a question of when, not if, Mozambique was to fall into the hands of FRELIMO.

THREE: UNDER SAS TERMS. 1973

Despite their less than fruitful dealings with the Portuguese military, the SAS didn't abandon operations in Mozambique. Aside from continuing to provide small numbers of men in the tracking and reconnaissance role in aid of local forces, C Squadron was determined to enter the fray independently of the Portuguese military. By 1973 ZANLA had established a firm foothold in the Tete province and was working alongside FRELIMO. While FRELIMO was still focussed on defeating the Portuguese, ZANLA was determined to use the area as a springboard for attacks into Rhodesia.

It took much careful negotiation with the Portuguese before they finally agreed to allow Rhodesian troops into the Tete province where they could attack ZANLA before they could enter Rhodesia. From the Portuguese perspective, the arrival of the SAS would herald a ramping up of the fight. They knew that, unlike them, the Rhodesian's were most proactive; seeking out the enemy and destroying him at every opportunity so, as soon as the C Squadron was allowed to 'slip the leash' things would get very noisy very quickly.

The first opportunity for the SAS to go external independently of the Portuguese came when a Rhodesian local government official was kidnapped by a ZANLA gang whilst on land surveying duties near the town of Mount Darwin, in the north-east of Rhodesia. There had been three white surveyors in the group, but two were killed in the initial ZANLA ambush. The black members of the surveying party were allowed to go free and later reported to the BSAP that they had overheard the ZANLA gang members saying that they intended to take their captive across the Zambezi into Mozambique. C Squadron was quickly alerted and an operation to free the man launched.

The SAS knew the locations of most of the various river crossing points on both the Zambezi and Musengezi rivers which were in use by ZANLA to get men in and out of the country. Time was of the essence if those responsible were to be intercepted before they could disappear into the hinterland of the Tete province. C Squadron was to deploy in as much strength as could be mustered and would go into action by both static-line and freefall parachute. It was to be C Squadron's first operational parachute drop since Malaya.

Two four-man callsigns were to act as pathfinders, each deploying to either side of the Musengezi River, some thirty-five miles inside Mozambique. They were to be delivered using HALO (High Altitude Low Opening) freefall from a RhAF Dakota transport plane flying at 18,000 feet. Given the speed that the operation was put together, usual parachuting protocols had to be set aside for the main body of operators who would be arriving later. There were no suitable DZs (Drop Zones) within the vicinity into which static-line parachutists could be delivered, so the SAS simply selected the largest and most open area of ground they could and hoped for the best.

One of the leaders of the pathfinder teams was Lieutenant Chris Schollenberg. *At this point I feel it necessary to make note of the legend that was 'Schulie'. Born in South Africa, he joined the Rhodesian Light Infantry where he served as a Sergeant before being commissioned as a Second Lieutenant. Lt Schollenberg then volunteered for the SAS, passing selection before joining C Squadron. In an atmosphere where excellence was the norm, he soon began to stand out from his SAS comrades, earning a reputation for himself by virtue of his daring exploits while on reconnaissance duties (it was later said by Lieutenant Colonel Ron Reid-Daly that*

"Schulie was without doubt the foremost exponent of reconnaissance in the Rhodesian Army ... perhaps in the world ... and the techniques he had developed had enabled the Selous Scouts' Reconnaissance Troop to carry out incredibly detailed reconnaissance's of targets deep inside Zambia and Mozambique. The two man reconnaissance concept, which I had initially viewed with the utmost doubt and concern, had proved to be such a success that we did not consider any target on the African continent, that was within Dakota range, to be beyond our capabilities."

After leaving the SAS at the end of his contract of service, Chris returned to South Africa but returned to Rhodesia where he joined the newly raised Selous Scouts. The reputation he earned with the SAS preceded him and was replicated, and extended, during his time with the Scouts.

He was only one of two men to be awarded the Grand Cross of Valour (The Rhodesian equivalent of the Victoria Cross or Congressional Medal of Honour) during the bush war.

It was daytime and the pathfinders were extremely heavily loaded as they boarded the Dakota which was to carry them out to their respective DZs, so much so that they had to be helped aboard by the RhAF dispatchers. The Plane took off and climbed hard to gain altitude before settling down on a course which would take them out towards Mozambique. Given the height, everyone aboard was obliged to wear oxygen masks.

As they approached the first drop zone a light ground haze had settled across the area, making it difficult for the RhAF crew to pick out the relevant navigation points but, exercising considerable skill, they managed to find the correct spot. Soon the men of the first pathfinder team were up and going through their pre-jump routines; checking their own and each other's kit for anything which may cause problems after they left the aircraft. By now, the SAS men had divested themselves of their oxygen masks and were becoming prone to losing consciousness in the thin high altitude air.

With the green light came the order to jump and the men were out of the Dakota in a tight stick. As they fell to earth it became clear that one of their number was in trouble; he was seen tumbling wildly away from the main group to disappear towards the ground. Those who watched the unfolding drama could only hope that their friend had managed to correct his descent and opened either his main or reserve 'chute out of their sight. Canopies were deployed at 2,500 feet but, as hard as everyone looked, there was no sign of missing man.

A few moments later the second callsign were deposited high above their own target. Fortunately they all made it down without incident. Up in the Dakota, Lieutenant Brian Robinson (he who led the aborted attack on the ZAPU HQ in Lusaka) was monitoring the situation. He was waiting for messages from the two pathfinder teams telling him all was going to plan. Instead, his blood chilled when Chris Schollenberg broke across the airwaves.

"This is Papa One." He said. "One of my men has gone straight into the ground."

After a brief exchange with Schollenberg and another call from the second pathfinder team which confirmed they were all down safely, the Dakota turned for home.

Lieutenant Schollenberg turned his attention away from pathfinding duties in order to mount a search for the missing man. Time was against him as he and the two remaining team members scoured to bush. Eventually, they had to abort the search. The man was nowhere to be found and the main body of SAS were due to arrive.

It was during the last hour of the day that the rest of the unit dropped into the makeshift DZ. Both pathfinder teams had done their best to find a suitable location for the drop but none were available. When the Dakota arrived overhead hurried exchanges between it and the pathfinders ensued. Lieutenant Schollenberg reported that, on his side of the river, the area was covered in trees. Over on the far bank, the other officer had slightly better news insofar as he'd managed to locate a DZ of sorts; an open area of ground; the downside being that it was littered with rocks. While still unsuitable in terms of size and hazards, it was clear that it offered a better chance for everyone to get down safely than the prospect of jumping into trees. C Squadron had done plenty of the latter while in Malaya, when there was simply no other way of inserting troops into remote jungle locations and had suffered a disproportionate injury rate as a result. Jumping in the dark, when there was no chance of correctly identifying obstacles and perhaps even steering the 'chutes away a little meant it was out of the question. A quick choice was made and it was decided that both sticks would drop into the 'safer' DZ. They made the jump and, aside from one man who suffered a broken ankle, no injuries were incurred.

Not long afterwards, and quite by chance, the body of Lieutenant Schollenberg's colleague was found. It was recovered to where it could be removed by helicopter back to Rhodesia and care was taken not to disturb the partially deployed parachute as everyone knew it would serve as vital evidence in the inevitable military inquiry.

Eventually, An Alouette III came on scene. Flying low and with its navigation and landing lights off, its pilot somehow managed to find a spot where it was just permissible to make a landing. Given the darkness and nature of the terrain, it was a risky manoeuvre. The body was placed aboard and the chopper lifted off, turning towards Rhodesia as it rose above the trees.

Over on the far bank, as the SAS were splitting up into their respective callsigns for deployment, the men who were to join Lieutenant Schollenberg faced their own problem. Because they'd been forced to use the other DZ they were on the wrong side of the Musengezi River.

Arriving on the bank they were met by a one hundred and twenty yard wide body of water which was in full flow. The rains had been and turned the usually placid river into a seemingly un-navigable torrent. The officer in charge told his men to search the riverbank for something they could use to assist their passage and, incredibly, not all that far away they found an old dugout canoe. It was quickly concluded that the canoe was nothing to do with ZANLA, but had been washed down river during an earlier flood.

As part of their training, the SAS were taught how to handle boats and cross rivers by way of swimming; subsequently, every man was a strong swimmer and what may have been an impassable barrier to most, was not so daunting to the SAS. It was still dangerous though, and everyone knew that the fast flowing water could easily sweep a man to his death.

The men stripped off their clothes and put them and their Bergens into the canoe before plunging into the maelstrom of water. Everyone made the far bank without incident, as did the canoe, clothes were recovered and they set out to rendezvous with Lieutenant Schollenberg's party.

As dawn broke over the area, all the SAS callsigns were at their respective start points. The operation called for all the SAS callsigns involved to mount a sweep of the area in search of the terrorists and their captive. They were looking for spoor; tracks and other sign which would lead them to their targets, however, the biblical downpours which are the African rains meant that the task of identifying trails became increasingly difficult. As well as the spoor being literally washed away, the SAS men were constantly soaked to the skin and, even though their Bergens had waterproof covers, so was all their kit.

A few days into the operation one of the callsigns spotted two armed men. Their assault rifles marked them both out as terrorists as opposed to civilians or poachers. The SAS allowed them to close before opening fire. One of the men was killed instantly while the other managed a miraculous escape; fleeing headlong into the bush at terrific speed after dropping his rifle. The search of the body recovered a letter from FRELIMO high command which instructed local units to allow the ZANLA kidnap gang and their captive to pass through the area unmolested.

Although they didn't know it at the time, the SAS had missed the ZANLA gang. The combination of the bad weather and not having enough men on the ground to search the area effectively meant they had slipped the net.

Eventually, when it became clear that the terrorists weren't going to be found, the SAS were withdrawn. In two separate contacts they had accounted for three FRELIMO killed. After being copied, photographs and the documentation carried by the terrorists were passed on to the Portuguese authorities as proof that FRELIMO were operating in an area which was hitherto unknown to them and the Rhodesian's.

As far as the SAS were concerned, valuable lessons had been learned. Unbeknown to all concerned, this was at the very start of the bush war and C Squadron was still feeling its way forward. Those same lessons were to be applied to future missions to make the SAS more effective when it came to operating in the harsh environs of the bush.

As for the kidnapped civilian – who was a British citizen living and working in Rhodesia – he was transported some 1,000 miles until he was eventually imprisoned in Tanzania. ZANU got much propaganda value from the kidnap and the prospect that the same fate may await them unsettled quite a few foreign workers in Rhodesia. *In this case the British government intervened and secured the man's release after he'd spent over twelve months in prison.*

FOUR: ON THE OFFENSIVE. 1974

The nature of the war had changed since the early days. By 1972 the conflict was in full swing. Acknowledging that their tactics had been largely unsuccessful, both ZANLA and ZIPRA had adapted accordingly. Instead of putting large groups of men across the border into Rhodesia, groups who by their very nature were easy to track and interdict, the terrorists were now using smaller sized gangs; sometimes numbering single-figures and putting more of them into Rhodesia at any one time in the hope of overwhelming the scant resources available to the Rhodesian's.

From the Rhodesian perspective, much valuable experience had been gained and none more than among the men of the SAS. By 1974 Brian Robinson was the new CO of C Squadron. He's been with the SAS for some years and, prior to UDI, had been seconded to serve with 22 SAS in the UK. It was normal for personnel from the overseas SAS units to go on attachment with the British regiment so his appointment wasn't out of the ordinary. Apart from learning new skills which could then be applied among their respective parent Squadrons, the British SAS were also able to absorb the talents which were unique to those from other parts of the world that may prove useful in time of conflict or during low-level covert 22 SAS operations in far flung corners of the globe.

Right up until his own appointment as C Squadron commander, the SAS had concentrated on reconnaissance operations. They were the eyes and ears of the army, building up comprehensive pictures of enemy movements and locations whenever they were called upon to do so. With one eye on his experience with 22 SAS, the now Major Robinson was determined to give C Squadron a more offensive role in the fight against the communist terrorist forces which threatened Rhodesia's very existence.

C Squadron had been increasingly heavily engaged in Mozambique's Tete province, assisting a Portuguese administration which was teetering on the edge of collapse but, as the conflict wore on, they found their services were required in other areas and often as a matter of urgency. Being such a small unit, the SAS found itself perpetually overstretched. The army wanted them to be everywhere all the time and, although C Squadron always tried its best to oblige, it was simply an impossibility.

ZIPRA had been building up its offensive capabilities and by the early 1970s was not only putting terror gangs into Rhodesia from Zambia, but was infiltrating via Botswana (though on a much smaller scale). The hub of the terrorist effort was the many training and holding camps they had established in the southern areas of Zambia.

Documents which were captured during a camp attack suggested there was a larger ZIPRA facility not all that far away from the one the RLI had just removed from the map. Despite extensive RhAF reconnaissance sorties over the area, no sign of any such camp was visible. It was decided that what was needed was boots on the ground to appraise the situation and confirm or deny the existence of such a facility.

C Squadron was tasked with locating this mysterious camp. In a change of direction, Major Robinson wanted C Squadron to be responsible for not only locating and reconnoitring this new target, but also completing its destruction.

Lieutenant Schollenberg and three men were tasked to go in locate then find everything out about this suspected new terrorist camp. They dressed for the operation in typical ZIPRA attire, carrying AK-47s and wearing captured ZIPRA webbing. The disguise was complete by the use of 'Black is Beautiful' cream, a theatrical type paint which when applied to white skin made it appear black. Because the area was alive with terrorists and Zambian army, it was not feasible to insert using helicopter, instead the callsign would infiltrate by boat across the Zambezi. Under cover of darkness, the SAS men were deposited on the Zambian bank. Moving carefully to avoid the local fishermen who were camped at various points along the river, Lieutenant Schollenberg and his team negotiated their way slowly towards their final destination, some five miles away. Moving tactically all the way to avoid being seen or heard, the callsign eventually reached the area they had been tasked to search. It was a very dark night so they were using their noses and their ears to tell them if there were any terrorists present. Inside friendly territory, noise discipline was not a concern for ZIPRA. As a result it would not be unusual to hear things that would otherwise not be heard in the bush. Movement, conversation, laughter, even singing would carry a long way in the still night air, as would the smell of wood smoke or cooking. Before they arrived on station they did encounter a couple of ZIPRA gangs but these, they concluded, were just routine movements and could not be connected to the illusive camp.

Lying up by day in positions which would afford the best view of the surrounding area as possible and moving by night, the team made steady progress through the search area. It was on the third night of the patrol that Lieutenant Schollenberg's team came across their first hard evidence of a human presence in the search area. They had heard gunfire in the distance and their experience told them that the shots were fired from high powered rifles. They suspected – correctly – that some ZIPRA were out on a hunting expedition to get meat for the cooking pot; could it be men from the camp they were searching for? On high alert lest they inadvertently bump into anyone else, the callsign eased their way towards where they suspected the camp might be situated. Here, a sudden contact – even if it didn't result in gunfire – would spell disaster for the SAS. They would have to break from whoever had spotted them and clear the area before ZIPRA could descend in force to kill or capture them. They were on their own, with no prospect of rescue from the air; to fly a chopper in to a place where there may be hundreds – if not thousands – of heavily armed terrorists just waiting to open fire on it would be to invite disaster.

After finding a suitable place to hide, the callsign settled down to ride out the coming day. They believed they were close enough to the suspected camp to be able to determine once and for all if it actually existed.

Over the next hours they heard and saw vehicular movement; light and heavy trucks travelling in several directions. They spotted two of the vehicles and noted that both were sporting olive green military style livery. They weren't Zambian army, neither were they civilian (at that point in time civilians in Zambia didn't own cars, let alone trucks and commercial vehicles would not be painted in that fashion). There were no points of habitation close enough to explain the trucks away as routine traffic; no, these were ZIPRA vehicles and it was time to confirm what they were up to. Lt Schollenberg left two men behind at the laying up point while he and the third man closed in on direction of the noise. They were moving very carefully now, across open country with only the long grass for cover. They could only move when the wind blew and the grass was swaying.

They'd not gone all that far when some shots rang out. Back at the LUP both men immediately assumed that the other two had been compromised so set about initiating the plan which would come into effect in the event of trouble. There was no word from the Lieutenant over the radio, so the two men pulled out and slowly made their way back to the ERV (Emergency Rendezvous) point where they hoped to meet up with the other half of the callsign. After waiting beyond the appointed cut-off time, they withdrew to the riverbank extraction point and summoned the boat.

The shots had come from somewhere, but it was nowhere near Lieutenant Schollenberg and his team mate. Unfortunately, due to an issue with their own transceiver, they had been unable to make contact with the men at the LUP to advise them to stay put.

After lying up in cover as close to the camp as they dared, and now knowing that the other half of the callsign would have followed procedures and withdrawn, Lieutenant Schollenberg remained determined to carry on with the operation. He and his companion found somewhere to hide out the rest of the day then settled down to wait.

During the early hours of the following morning, under cover of a moonless night's sky, the men moved forward once more until they began to see signs of an enemy base. This wasn't marked on any of their maps; could it be the mystery camp? Carefully, they penetrated the perimeter and found themselves in the camp proper. Though there was much evidence of previous occupation, it soon became apparent that the place was deserted. This could indeed be the place that was alluded to in the captured documents but the SAS had arrived too late to make any capital.

After withdrawing they sent an encoded Morse message to SAS HQ. As far as Chris Schollenberg was concerned, although this camp was empty, his instinct was telling him that there was sure to be another in use somewhere close by. Permission was granted to extend the search and, the following night, the two men recommenced their hunt. After spotting a small group of men sitting round a camp fire, they continued their hunt.

A night of hard work had seen them draw a blank; the plan now was to find some high ground upon which they could observe comings and goings throughout the immediate vicinity and they happened upon such a place while it was still dark. Often, what may seem like a good place to lay up in the darkness often turns out to be the complete opposite in daylight but, on this occasion luck was with them. They could remain in good cover and were able to see over an area for many hundreds of yards in almost every direction.

During the following day the men saw several fully armed ZIPRA travelling by bicycle along a dirt track which they suspected to also be in use by the elusive trucks. A couple of likely looking points which were ideal locations for a secret camp had drawn Lieutenant Schollenberg's attention and that night he decided he would investigate further, however that and subsequent searches drew a blank.

With the SAS leadership deciding they were searching for something which simply wasn't there, Lieutenant Schollenberg was ordered out of the area. When he arrived back at Cranborne his continued insistence that the captured terrorist documentation was correct and there was an as yet undiscovered ZIPRA camp somewhere within the vicinity meant that within a matter of weeks he was back.

This time the young officer was accompanied by two SAS NCOs. They infiltrated by boat across the Zambezi, landing in the same location as before, and just like last time, they were disguised as ZIPRA.

The callsign carefully navigated their way into the target area, noting that several tracks they crossed while doing so contained spoor made by Soviet issue army boots (which were issued to ZIPRA).

A few days into the patrol, and having come into close proximity of civilians and ZIPRA alike but not finding any evidence of a terrorist camp, the SAS team came to a point which had been marked out for their attention. The feature was a large square hole which had shown up on recent RhAF reconnaissance photographs. It was suspected that the terrorists were in the process of constructing an underground arms cache and it was possible that it could be part of the phantom ZIPRA camp. It was up to Chris Schollenberg to confirm or dismiss it. By now, whoever was digging the hole had decided to attempt to hide it from the air by stretching camouflage netting across both it and the area immediately surrounding it. This had alerted all concerned on the Rhodesian side and they concluded that ZIPRA was up to no good at the site.

As the team approached the location of the mysterious hole they were met with the sound of activity. Sawing, hammering and even singing; someone was busy constructing something alright but the team would have to get much closer before they could get eyes on the target. Closing through the long grass and only moving when the wind blew so as to disguise their movement in the swaying grass, the callsign eased themselves into a position where they could observe exactly what was going on. Sure enough, a large group of men were hard at work in and around the hole. Parked up close by under cover of the surrounding trees was a truck painted in olive green. It wasn't a Zambian army vehicle, so had to be ZIPRA. Although most of the men were out of sight as they toiled inside the hole, it was obvious to the callsign that they were engaged in major construction work. The SAS observed that the construction crew were being most careful to dump the displaced soil (of which there appeared to be many tons from that day's work alone) under the trees where its different colour couldn't be spotted by passing aircraft.

After keeping the target under observation for the remainder of the day, Lieutenant Schollenberg and his team concluded that the RhAF suspicions were indeed correct; ZIPRA were in the process of constructing an underground bunker, and a big one at that, into which they could store a large number of weapons and other associated equipment, what's more, from other activity they'd observed within the immediate vicinity, it was clear that the terrorists were also building a new camp to go with this arms dump.

After dark, the SAS team withdrew and made their way back to the Zambezi, anti-tracking all the way and being extra careful not to come into contact with any roving bands of ZIPRA in the darkness. They reached the extraction point without incident and were picked up and removed to Rhodesia by boat.

They'd brought back a wealth of intelligence regarding the under construction arms cache and the building of the new camp itself, including photographs and detailed hand drawn sketch maps.

When the findings of Lieutenant Schollenberg's reconnaissance mission were shared with Brigade HQ (at that point in time, C Squadron was a Brigade asset and not under the direct control of Rhodesian High Command) the officer in charge was displeased that the SAS had not chosen to attack the target after its discovery. It was pointed out that to attack the camp before it was finished and occupied would be a waste of resources. The SAS intended to bide their time until all the terrorist weapons had been stored in the underground bunker, that way they would be in a position to deny ZIPRA the ability to arm and resupply a lot of their Rhodesian bound terror gangs. Another bonus of waiting would come by way of the SAS also having the opportunity to kill the terrorists who would then be occupying the adjoining camp.

Over the coming weeks, several RhAF high altitude reconnaissance overflights of the area were mounted and the progress of the construction carefully monitored. It was eventually reported that the hole had disappeared completely beneath a thatched roof and more camouflage netting. This was a sure sign that the building work was complete and enemy were preparing to stock it with small arms, ammunition, RPG-7s, mines, and other assorted ordnance destined for use against civilian and infrastructure targets in Rhodesia.

Another recce callsign was inserted into the area to confirm what the RhAF photographic interpreters were telling them and, after said confirmation arrived, the SAS set about planning to attack the site.

Some forty-two men (almost all C Squadron) were to be involved in the operation, including the acting CO, Captain Barratt (Major Robinson was recovering from a bout of serious illness and was not fit for duty). From the beginning it was taken for granted that they would find themselves outnumbered yet, in typical Rhodesian fashion, the odds being stacked against them was no deterrent.

C Squadron Assembled at a Forward Operating Base (FOB) on the Rhodesian side of the Zambezi. They brought enough Zodiac inflatable boats to ferry them across the river in one wave. Each of the Zodiacs were fitted with outboard engines which sported specially made exhaust systems which served to muffle the sound to levels which were acceptable for covert use. The SAS knew that the area was alive with native fishermen who would be quick to report any suspicious activity to the first passing Zambian army or police patrol.

The commander of the FOB was none other than Major Coventry, the former C Squadron CO who had led the first abortive external mission into Zambia. Major Coventry was now employed as a senior official with the CIO and he was keen to offer his full support to his old regiment.

There was no time to waste so, after everyone had been briefed and the layout of the target digested (courtesy of information provided by the last recce patrol), the SAS took to their boats for the crossing into Zambia. Up front, in the bow of the leading boat, one man had a special task. He'd been equipped with a night vision scope and his job was to scour the opposite bank for sign of human activity as the Zodiac's made the run in. Despite the specially adapted exhaust systems, the combined noise from the outboard motors was enough to cause concern as it would travel quite some way, possibly to the ears of nearby locals. Any Zambian fishermen who happened to be in the immediate vicinity who heard the boats would almost certainly report it to the authorities for reward money.

Fortunately, no one was about that night and the SAS raiding party landed without incident. They formed up then set off in single file along a route laid out for them by Chris Schollenberg.

Back at the FOB in Rhodesia it was another quiet night in the bush. The usual guard was mounted while everyone else turned in to get some sleep.

In the early hours the FOB came under sudden and totally unexpected attack. A small group of ZIPRA had converged upon the base before opening fire with automatic weapons. It was a brief yet violent assault, with ZIPRA withdrawing rapidly before the Rhodesian's could respond in kind. Two men were injured in the attack, one seriously, the other being Major Coventry who suffered a non-life threatening wound.

The realisation that ZIPRA was operating in such close proximity led the Rhodesian's to suspect that the SAS raiding party may have been spotted as they crossed the river, though at that point it was decided not to inform them in case Captain Barratt decided to abort the operation as a result.

The SAS were on schedule as they settled down into an LUP where they would rest and wait until after sundown.

The heat soon built and the day turned into a blistering example of what the African springtime could produce. Even though they were tired from the previous night's labours, the terrific heat meant that most men found it impossible to sleep.

After dark, the raiding party set off on the second leg of the journey. The march thus far has been circuitous, designed to separate the SAS from the prospect of bumping into civilians or ZIPRA. Lieutenant Schollenberg's navigation plan proved flawless and eventually the raiding party found themselves south-east of the target where they were to spilt up into their component parts. It wasn't simply a case of attacking the camp because the Rhodesian's knew from experience that as soon as things went noisy, the majority of ZIPRA would not hang around for a fight. Instead they'd bomb burst in every direction for the safety of the surrounding bush. It was for this reason that the SAS deployed 'stop groups' at strategic points. The job of these stop groups was to interdict the terrorists as they made their bid for freedom, ambushing them without warning and killing as many as possible in the process. For this particular mission there were to be three stop groups and two assault groups and, as the inhabitants of the camp slept soundly in the knowledge that they were safe from harm inside friendly territory, the SAS began the careful process of encirclement.

Captain Barratt was with one of the stop groups and monitored the progress of the raiders as they eased themselves into their respective positions. When the radio messages were received from each group telling him they were ready, it was time to go.

It was just starting to come light as Captain Barratt ordered the assault groups into action. They were deployed in two sweep lines and began their move north to south across the open area of the camp. Their first victim was a lone sentry; the man had been on duty for a while and had already been spotted by the hidden SAS as he mooched about the camp with his rifle hung lazily over his shoulder. He was cut down by a well aimed volley of fire and dead before he hit the dirt. That was the cue for the rest of the assault teams to begin shooting up the place in the hope of catching the stunned ZIPRA as they scrambled from their beds. By all accounts there was a terrific volume of automatic fire put down by the SAS as they continued to close on the enemy. Predictably, for their part, the ZIPRA campmates were only interested in one thing; escape. Some of the terrorists had the presence of mind to take their rifles, while others simply bolted headlong for the bush. Soon these survivors found themselves in the sights of the stop groups and were cut down as they ran.

Within five minutes of the opening shots being fired it was all over. The camp was in SAS hands and the process of destroying it and its secrets began. It was quickly realised that the camp was only home to a skeleton force of ZIPRA. With that in mind, Captain Barratt was hoping against hope that the underground arms dump wouldn't be empty.

While the stop groups and some of those involved in the assault went into all round defence to protect the scene from potential counter attack by either ZIPRA or the Zambian military, the rest began to search the camp. They were looking for anything of intelligence value which might prove of use to them, the CIO or Special Branch (the elite police anti-terrorist/intelligence unit).

The trapdoor entrance to the underground dump was found hidden beneath some carefully placed soil and two SAS men went down to investigate. What they found shocked the pair of them. There, in the earth was a concrete walled bunker almost twenty yards square! Despite Captain Barratt's doubts, the place was crammed full from floor to roof with all manner of armament and equipment, all neatly stacked for distribution to Rhodesian bound terrorists as and when it was required.

There were rifles, light and medium machineguns, sidearm's, grenades, anti-tank and anti-personnel landmines, explosives and detonation gear, RPG-7s and crated rockets, box upon box of ammunition and almost everything else which could be imagined which would be needed to fully equip a terrorist for offensive operations. It was noted that most of the weaponry was brand new and still crated up.

After taking a brief estimated inventory and some photographs for examination by the intelligence boys, the SAS set about rigging the bunker for demolition. The weaponry left behind by ZIPRA as the attack went in was deposited into the bunker where it too would be placed out of terrorist reach for good.

Time was now not on the side of the raiding party, the gunfire would have travelled to the surrounding villages and beyond, alerting civilians, terrorists and the Zambian authorities to the presence of Rhodesian troops.

With typical SAS devilment, some of the anti-tank mines were pulled from the bunker and laid on the track leading into the camp. It was hoped that when ZIPRA came to investigate events, one or more of their vehicles would be blown to pieces as a result.

Aside from what was found in the bunker, the rest of the camp yielded a lot of equipment. More explosives and detonation kits were found, as was a lot of food – the latter carefully stored for use over the coming months. Perhaps the most interesting find among the camp buildings was a detailed plan for a proposed attack on the Rhodesian School of Infantry in Gwelo, proof that these terrorists meant business and were prepared not to restrict themselves to 'soft' targets.

The buildings were set ablaze and soon the bunker readied for demolition. A slow burning fuse was initiated, giving the SAS chance to withdraw to a safe distance before the explosion occurred.

When it came, the violence of the explosion was such that it shocked even the SAS men. Ammunition, grenades and RPG rockets aside, there was estimated to be in excess of three tons of military grade plastic explosive contained within the target, when it went up the whole bunker was vaporised. Such was the event that the pall of smoke could be seen over fifty miles away in Rhodesia!

The temptation to remove rifles and pistols for future SAS use was too great and Captain Barratt ordered his men to carry out as much as they were able, the result being each man was very heavily loaded down as they began the withdrawal. It was still early but the heat was already building to put even more pressure of the weary SAS.

Despite the whole area being on the alert, the raiding party managed to stay out of sight during the exfiltration. It was a long, hard, move made in two legs with only a short stop off period to rest, but the rapidity of the withdrawal made sure they remained several steps ahead of any vengeful ZIPRA.

By the time the SAS reached the banks of the Zambezi they were all exhausted. The boats were summoned and appeared shortly afterwards to remove the men back to Rhodesia.

It had been the largest single SAS external mission of the war to date and a spectacular success for all involved. In one fell swoop C Squadron had removed the ability for ZIPRA to arm its men within a whole sector of operations. As a result of the destruction of the arms dump terrorist activity inside Matabeleland, Rhodesia, was severely curtailed for several months and it took even longer for ZIPRA to reorganise and re-equip themselves to pre-raid levels.

In recognition of the scale of the success of the operation, Captain Barratt was awarded the Order of the Legion of Merit, while for his efforts on both the raid and the reconnaissance missions, Chris Schollenberg won the Silver Cross of Rhodesia, the country's second highest gallantry award. His was the first Silver Cross given to an SAS operator.

FIVE: A CLOSE SHAVE. 1976

The SAS were now mounting numerous attacks against ZIPRA and ZANLA in both Zambia and Mozambique. At this point in time, the Portuguese had already withdrawn from Mozambique and FRELIMO had taken over control of the country. By allowing Robert Mugabe to station ZANLA there, the Rhodesian's worst fear had been realised; the dreaded second front had been opened up along the long and highly vulnerable land border between Rhodesia and Mozambique. This was a very serious problem for the Rhodesian security forces as, overstretched and under-resourced as they already were, the 'eastern front' meant that ZANLA were now able to infiltrate into Rhodesia almost at will.

In addition to offensive operations, reconnaissance and intelligence gathering remained a vital SAS task. In order for the army or air force to mount attacks on terrorist assets, they needed accurate and up to date information and it was to the SAS they looked to provide them with that same intelligence. It was dangerous work, carried out by small groups of lightly armed men who were often operating deep behind the lines and surrounded by hostile forces. They had little prospect of support, so one false move could spell disaster.

Of the countless examples of such SAS missions, the one which follows gives a glimpse into the risks the men involved took.

Rhodesian military intelligence had long suspected the presence of a ZANLA camp in an area not far away from the south-eastern border with Mozambique which was being used as springboard for terror gangs to enter the country and range deep into the Rhodesian interior. Despite their best efforts, the exact location of the camp proved a mystery. The only thing they were sure of was the fact that RhAF reconnaissance photographs showed that the whole area was alive with civilian activity. Numerous kraals were dotted about all over the area and every single inhabitant was violently pro-FRELIMO and ZANLA. Any Rhodesian's operating on the ground would find it extremely difficult to move without being compromised. If spotted by the locals, news of enemy troops would quickly carry back to FRELIMO and ZANLA which, in turn, would result in a reaction from both. With this in mind it was a most unhealthy place to be.

The Selous Scouts had been operating in the area but with limited success. The advantage the Scouts had over the SAS was the fact that many of its members were black. While SAS operators were forced to rely on 'Black is Beautiful' cream in an attempt to disguise their ethnicity, the Scouts could move with some measure of confidence. Apart from the obvious, Scouts were able to speak local tribal languages and were familiar with customs and routines so, even if they came within touching distance of any civilian, they'd often be able to talk their way out of trouble. That said, the local population were wise to that fact that the Rhodesian's were sending black troops into Mozambique, so any small groups of men seen out in the bush where it was unusual for friendly forces to normally operate – even if they were dressed as FRELIMO or ZANLA – were to be reported.

The Selous Scouts had been deployed into the area in search of the elusive ZANLA camp but on both occasions had found themselves compromised then forced to withdraw. If the Scouts were unable to successfully complete the tasking, it stood to reason that the SAS would have no more of a chance. That said, someone, somewhere decided to pass the baton on to C Squadron.

The order was clear; the SAS were to insert a reconnaissance callsign into the area and find the camp.

As soon as the tasking was received, everyone involved

knew it would be a tall order, even for the SAS. To give the mission a chance of success, it would be necessary to put the Squadron's best men onto the job.

When Lieutenant 'Mac' McIntosh was told to lead a four-man callsign in to find the elusive ZANLA camp he was sceptical of his chances of success. Pouring over the intelligence reports, maps and sheaves of RhAF reconnaissance photographs, it was immediately obvious that – even by SAS standards – his would be an unusually difficult assignment. If Rhodesia's other Special Forces unit, the superbly trained and deeply experienced Selous Scouts – had failed not once but twice, how could the SAS be expected to fare any better? Lieutenant McIntosh knew that to stand any chance of survival in that area he and his men would have to operate in disguise. It was something that he and the men he'd chosen to accompany him had previous experience of but, if the black Rhodesian Scouts operators couldn't pull it off, it would certainly prove impossible for him?

Lieutenant McIntosh selected his team; three men who were all seasoned SAS troops and well versed in the intricacies of operating under extremely challenging circumstances such as those they were sure to face.

After some brief but exhaustive preparation, the callsign was deposited into Mozambique by helicopter. They'd selected to HLZ carefully, making sure it was well south of the area to be searched and as clear of points of habitation as possible. Each man knew that, aside from spotting suspicious activity on the ground, the locals (and any ZANLA or FRELIMO patrols) would be on the lookout for air movements. Seeing or even hearing a helicopter was almost guaranteed to be reported. If this happened then it would be as good as game over. The already alert civilian population would be advised that Rhodesian soldiers were on the ground in the vicinity. Any compromise wouldn't necessarily come by way of the SAS being spotted, the locals knew the ground well and were able to pick up on spoor should they come across it. Many of them were able to read traces of movement where it would otherwise be invisible; to an experienced bushman, something as seemingly inconsequential as a turned leaf was a sign that someone had passed by. From reading tracks they could tell how many men were moving, how heavily loaded they were, and even how long since they had left the marks. If FRELIMO was able to collate this information using timings and direction of travel, they could quite easily interdict the interlopers at a point of their choosing. For this reason, the SAS would never travel 'point to point', all routes would be circuitous, doglegging seemingly erratically, not only to take advantage of the cover offered be trees or ground features, but to confuse any follow up.

As they moved off from the HLZ, Lieutenant McIntosh's party were most careful to make full use of dead ground and such, employing strict anti-tracking measures every step of the way. Moving so as not to leave sign meant they traded speed for caution, this was no issue as they weren't in a race; there were no deadlines to be met, the priority was not to be discovered.

Before long they began to see kraals. The inhabitants would have retired to bed but that didn't mean the SAS men could relax. Camp dogs were in abundance and their job was to be on the lookout for predators. If they saw or even got the scent of the callsign, they'd begin to bark and that barking would initiate a response from the locals.

There was no way of skirting the kraals, there were just too many, Lieutenant McIntosh's team had no alternative but to carefully pick their way through the often narrow areas of open ground which separated them.

As the sun began to rise, the SAS found the kraals to their backs; that they'd managed to negotiate that most difficult of obstacles without being compromised was a testament to their skill. The priority now was to find somewhere where they could lay up for the hours of daylight. They were still within visual range of the kraals and the likelihood of locals passing in close proximity was all too real. The callsign knew they had to go to ground before the civilians began to emerge and there was little time left for them to do it. Frustratingly, the area was flat and devoid of any semblance of cover. A scrap of dead ground was the best they could find and they deposited themselves into it. It was far from ideal but, unless they sat up, they knew they would go unseen by anyone close by.

The men were exhausted from their exertions; it wasn't only the physical but the mental strain of being constantly alert for hours on end which took its toll, that said, there was no time to relax. Routines had to be observed. The first priority was to get a radio message away to Rhodesia to inform SAS commanders that all was going according to plan. Given the precarious nature of the LUP, the signaller couldn't use the usual antennae set-up, instead a wire aerial had to be coiled along the ground around the perimeter of the hideout and fiddled with endlessly before a link could be established. Then men had to eat, 'hard routine' was the order of the day. There was absolutely no possibility of cooking anything as the smell would drift on the breeze before finding its way into the keen nostrils of the locals.

After attending to these matters and more only then could the callsign settle down to get some rest. One man was to remain on sentry duty, rotating with the others at set intervals.

The day dragged by, on several occasions the callsign was brought to the alert by the sound of the kraals folk as they went about their chores. While the SAS couldn't chance taking a peek out of cover, it was estimated that the civilians came as close as fifty yards to the LUP. The 'actions on' plan in the event of compromise had been worked out after the callsign's arrival. They'd move north into an area which afforded cover, before cutting away on several tangents so as to confuse the FRELIMO follow up operation. If they became split, they'd head for the ERV and wait for the others to join them.

At long last darkness fell over the scene and after waiting until they were sure they wouldn't be spotted, the callsign eased themselves slowly from cover and began the second leg of the journey into the area suspected as being the location of the ZANLA camp.

Spending the day lying down and unable to even sit up meant the men were stiff, but the aches and pains were soon forgotten as they probed forwards towards the objective. They'd been most careful not to leave any sign of their presence behind. The LUP was searched to make sure it was clear (the callsign even took their bodily waste with them to dump somewhere out of sight in the bush) before it was abandoned.

That night's night march was equally arduous but, on the plus side, there were a few less kraals to be negotiated.

As daybreak came on the second day, the callsign found itself on the rather steep slope of a small kopje (hill). The surrounding area was a mixture of scrub and open grassland, with trees dotted about hither and thither. This, they concluded, was about a good a place to lay up as they were going to find. They settled into position by the base of a tree; the surrounding scrub meant they were hidden from view so they felt relatively secure for the first time since leaving Rhodesia. The tree would prove a useful vantage point with which to observe the area so Lieutenant McIntosh sent one of the men up into its higher branches with a pair of binoculars to scour the landscape and maintain a guard.

They were now at the start point for the mission proper. That night they'd begin the search for the elusive ZANLA camp.

At around mid-morning, the man who'd taken over sentry duty up the tree was amazed to see a small group of fully armed ZANLA emerge from the scrub. They were danger close to the LUP and closing on it almost as if they suspected it was there. He was shocked as he had neither seen nor heard them approach. Unusually for the terrorists, they were observing strict noise discipline as they made their way forward. Within a few paces they were directly under the tree and stood there in silence. Up in the branches, the sentry looked on, hoping against hope that he wouldn't be spotted. Over on the other side of the tree, his three comrades were sound asleep in the shade. If the ZANLA men stepped to either side just a couple of yards or so, they would spot the three SAS men. At such close quarters and, despite the Black is Beautiful cream, it would be immediately obvious that they were looking at white men wearing ZANLA uniforms. They'd have the drop on the sleeping callsign but, before they could do anything about it, they didn't realise that one wrong move would have seen them come under fire from above. With luck, the sentry thought, he'd buy enough time for his colleagues to grab for their weapons and begin shooting, driving off the enemy long enough for him to return to earth.

A tense few minutes passed and the sentry hardly dare breathe as he looked on from the treetop. Eventually, the ZANLA group moved away, equally silently, into the scrub. After making sure they were gone, and double checking the immediate area, the sentry scrambled to the ground to alert the others. Lieutenant McIntosh was stunned at the news. A quick conflab followed and it was agreed that there was no other reason for ZANLA to be there other than they were looking for Rhodesian troops. Somehow, somewhere, they must have been spotted as they were moving during the night. This being the case they knew that the ZANLA group who'd almost walked straight into them wouldn't be alone. Given the fact that they were moving tactically, creating no noise and using the ground to its best advantage, there could be dozens of such groups out scouring the area in search of them. If the enemy were following up their spoor, which despite their best anti-tracking efforts, they had to assume to be the case, it would only be a question of time before the callsign was discovered.

It was still early and there were many hours of daylight left. To move under cover of night was difficult enough, but to attempt it during daylight in such close proximity to hostile civilians and enemy forces?!

Lieutenant McIntosh made the decision. They could not stay here. He quickly told the men the bones of a plan. They already knew the location of the ERV so, if the worst happened and they got split, they would meet up there and get the hell out of the area. As far as the mission was concerned, it was scrubbed. They'd been compromised so the priority now was a successful evasion to a point where they could be extracted by helicopter.

Lieutenant McIntosh wanted to put in a call to Rhodesia on the emergency frequency to tell of their predicament so that a chopper could be readied to lift them to safety, but he decided that would have to wait. They needed to go, and go quickly.

Just as the men were pulling on their Bergens, all hell let loose. The entire area around the tree was suddenly saturated with gunfire. Rifles and machineguns raked the scene, the bullet strikes causing the earth to erupt. Fortunately for the SAS men, the tree was between them and mush of the shooting so they were sheltered from the worst of it by its thick trunk. The amount of incoming was such that the callsign was unable to move. At first the SAS men thought they had been pinpointed but, as the fire swept past them, they quickly realised that the enemy didn't know exactly where they were. It was obvious that the enemy was attempting to draw the SAS into shooting back. So long as the callsign held their own fire, ZANLA would continue to blindly rake the area. Once the shooting swept past them again, they would make their move, travelling quickly but tactically over the ridgeline and onto the reverse slope. By now the gunfire had been joined by RPG-7 rockets which exploded to all sides. It was getting decidedly unhealthy!

At the first opportunity the callsign made its move, scrambling up and over the ridge without being seen. The biggest problem now would come if ZANLA had the presence of mind to contain the area around the LUP.

No sooner had they reached the safety of the reverse slope than they came under fire from several points in the bush. Now the SAS realised they'd been cut off as ZANLA had indeed been tactically aware enough to make sure they surrounded the kopje. Pulling back over the slope, the callsign scrambled into cover. The radio operator managed to get a signal off informing SAS HQ of their predicament and requesting immediate extraction. They knew time was of the essence if they were to escape from the situation they now found themselves in.

Bad news was sent in return; there were no helicopters available at that time and, although the RhAF was giving the incident the utmost priority, they could not estimate when they'd be able to mount a sortie to rescue the callsign.

By now things were becoming really serious for the SAS team. A quick survey of the area confirmed their worst fears; ZANLA had moved into position in large numbers and were encircling their position. The searching fire continued as thousands of rounds were being fired into anywhere the terrorists thought Rhodesian's might be hiding. As well as the odd RPG-7 round, the blizzard of incoming fire had been joined by a mortar barrage. Ricochet's and white hot shrapnel were whining all around but still the SAS held their fire. Given the weight of fire which ZANLA were able to put down, it was vital that they remain unseen. Lieutenant McIntosh and his team knew they were being softened up for the next phase of the ZANLA operation. The enemy wouldn't sit there all day expending countless tens of thousands of rounds at targets they couldn't see, before long the indiscriminate shooting would be replaced by an infantry style assault. The objective would be to kill or capture the SAS team and bring the terrorist mission to a conclusion.

Before long the shooting died down. To their rear, on the reverse slope, the callsign began to hear whistle blasts and shouts. The enemy was moving up the slope to clear it of the Rhodesian's. ZANLA still didn't know whereabouts on the hill the SAS men were hiding so were exercising extreme caution as they advanced lest they run into an ambush.

This was it, as soon as the enemy appeared on the ridge, the callsign would let them have it. They were only equipped with AK-47s but – on auto – they could still put down a withering weight of fire. They also knew that the terrorists on their side of the slope would be unable to shoot for fear of hitting their own men. Each operator knew they would have to exercise extreme aggression if they were to survive the coming fight; severely outnumbered and outgunned, the SAS men were prepared to take the fight to the enemy. They planned to counter attack, sweeping ZANLA off the ridge with automatic rifle fire and grenades. They'd probably be outnumbered ten to one but were determined to send the enemy running back down to their start points. It would then be a case of trying to melt back into the scrub and hide from view as the terrorists on their side of the slope recommenced their shooting.

As they waited to go into action, the patrol radio crackled into life. It was the SAS. Although there were still no choppers available, the RhAF personnel responsible had been warned that if they didn't do something – and do it fast – some C Squadron boys would descend on the FOB to 'knock their bloody blocks off'.

It was cold comfort for Lieutenant McIntosh and his team. It was obvious they couldn't hang on for much longer; it was a miracle that none of them had been killed already but, as events was playing out, that was only a question of time.

For some reason, the expected attack from the far side of the slope never materialised. Instead of storming the SAS men, the enemy simply returned to the relative safety of their positions among the scrub at the base of the slope.

After it became clear that the danger from the other side of the ridge had passed, Lieutenant McIntosh instructed his men to dump their Bergens and fill their pouches and pockets with ammunition and supplies which would sustain them in the bush. They also checked each other's Black is Beautiful to make sure it was holding up in the heat. Ideally, they'd wait until well after dark before attempting what he had in mind but, seeing as they wouldn't be afforded the luxury of waiting that long, he'd already decided that he'd lead his callsign off the kopje in an attempt to break though ZANLA lines and out into the bush beyond. It was desperate stuff, and no doubt the terrorists were expecting it but, if they stayed put, they'd be killed anyway. Using their training they might just be able to sneak past ZANLA but the likeliest outcome would be the need to mount an attack on whoever got in their way, fire and manoeuvring forwards using speed, aggression and surprise. Using fragmentation and smoke grenades to blast their way through and cover their flanks. They'd have to move hard and fast, perhaps for many miles before they broke away from ZANLA so the only substantial kit to be taken was the patrol radio and some spare batteries.

Following the Lieutenant's instruction, the callsign's

radioman made contact with Rhodesia once more to pass a situation report. He made no bones about communicating the dire situation the SAS team were now in. To everyone's anger, it was reported that still no helicopters were available, but an RhAF Lynx light ground attack plane, fresh from the same fireforce engagement which was consuming all the local rotary wing capabilities, had landed at a FAF (forward airfield) and was being refuelled and rearmed then would be on standby to provide support should the callsign require it. Should the callsign require it?! The Lynx (known as the Cessna O-2A Skymaster in USAF service) was a propeller driven light aircraft which the RhAF used to great effect. It could carry all manner of light ordnance, from machineguns, to rocket pods and small fragmentation and napalm bombs. Having it appear above the SAS team could make the difference between survival and death.

Now the shooting to their front died away. This could only mean one thing. Lieutenant McIntosh told his men to stand by to repel a frontal attack. Digging themselves into cover from fire and view, the four men waited. Soon afterwards a group of ZANLA burst from the scrub, they were in a tight group (which was good news for the SAS) and working their way quickly up the slope. Lieutenant McIntosh let them come on before initiating the contact with a burst of automatic fire from his Kalashnikov. Waiting for his cue, the others joined in. Several terrorists were cut down in the initial volleys. The enemy returned inaccurate fire as they began a haphazard retreat back downhill and a couple more were killed in the process.

That was it, Lieutenant McIntosh concluded, it was now time to go.

After the expected ZANLA attack from the far side of the slope failed to materialise, Lieutenant McIntosh had sent one of his team up to the ridgeline to see what was happening. The man had made a detailed appreciation of the ZANLA positions and deduced that there was enough of a gap between two of them to allow the SAS to escape.

In the brief slack period, while ZANLA were withdrawing and their comrades were unable to recommence firing for fear of hitting their own men, the Lieutenant was aware they could move without being fired upon. Staying under cover and moving tactically, the callsign made their way up and over the crest. They had to be extra careful now as one false move would reveal their location to the watching ZANLA on the far slope.

There was no shooting here, ZANLA knew that their comrades had just made contact with the Rhodesian's and were waiting hear of the outcome.

The four men descended cautiously, using the scrub as cover and being careful not to raise dust, until they found themselves at the base of the slope. There was still cover to their front but they knew it opened up as it came to the ZANLA positions. Lieutenant McIntosh made sure everyone was okay before ordering the next move. Behind them, the shooting had recommenced as the ZANLA assault group withdrew to safety.

The callsign began to move forward, they were all on high alert and expecting to be challenged at any second. A shout or a shot would have seen then bounding forwards, fire and manoeuvring towards then through the enemy line. Although the instinct was to run, the men had to control themselves.

Soon they were in an area of open ground and exposed to view from all directions, they hadn't gone far when they saw movement to their left. A small group of ZANLA were ensconced in a patch of scrub about thirty yards away. They made no sudden moves as the SAS men passed by; it quickly became apparent that, as far as the terrorists were concerned, these four men were comrades. The callsign kept walking, as nonchalantly as possible, until they found themselves in the embrace of a dense patch of scrub. They'd made it! Their ZANLA uniforms and Black is Beautiful had worked, and in daylight too!

With the ZANLA positions now behind them the SAS were determined to capitalise on their sudden good fortune. There was to be no finesse about the next phase of 'operation breakout', it would simply be a case of putting as much distance as possible between themselves and the terrorists as possible before the latter realised the Rhodesian's had slipped their net. Anti-tracking was out, for the time being at least, after all and despite their best efforts, ZANLA had been able to hunt them down to their LUP.

The men set off at a run and knew they wouldn't stop until they'd cleared the area.

After a while Lieutenant McIntosh ordered a halt. The callsign needed to assess their situation. Against all odds they'd escaped what would otherwise have been certain death, but they weren't out of the frying pan yet. The area they now found themselves in was devoid of any cover for many hundreds of yards in every direction. It was mostly turned over to the growing of crops and that – and the huts dotted about – meant they'd be encountering civilian activity all the way. A brief radio message was sent to Rhodesia to inform the SAS and RhAF of their current situation. Amazingly, there were still no helicopters available to airlift them to safety. The callsign agreed among themselves that whatever battle the security forces were engaged in, it must be a bloody big one!

After checking their disguises and setting the route and all important ERV, the SAS men set off once more. Given the nature of the ground and the almost inevitable chance of being seen, the callsign decided not to run. While their close encounter with ZANLA proved they could pass themselves off as terrorists, to run would immediately arouse suspicion and, quite possibly, be reported. When ZANLA realised the Rhodesian's had escaped, part of the inevitable search would be to ask questions among the locals. The four mysterious 'ZANLA' men would be spoken about and the hunt narrowed accordingly. Until then, the SAS would buy themselves more time by acting normally.

It wasn't long into the move that the callsign began to see civilians. The locals had seen them and the SAS men were heartened as each one waved at what they believed to be their ZANLA allies. Meandering so as not to get too close to anyone, the callsign made its way through the fields of burnt maize stubble.

Their next waypoint was on the edge of the fields, a small rocky outcrop which marked the boundary them and what lay beyond. Instead of the crop fields, this distant area of open ground appeared to be in use as grazing land.

As the SAS men approached they could see a hut some hundred yards to their half-right. No one appeared to be out and about in the immediate vicinity. They'd almost made it through another dangerous obstacle. After leaving the fields behind, they were confident they'd be able to pick up the pace once more.

As the callsign came to the outcrop they suddenly found themselves under intense automatic fire. ZANLA had hidden themselves around the hut and opened up with several light machineguns as the SAS came into ambush range. The SAS scrambled for cover in amongst the rocks, hundreds of rounds chasing them as they went. Amazingly, and given the volume of fire, none of the callsign was hurt. They ran clear, clambering out of sight onto the far side of the outcrop. ZANLA were still shooting but the SAS were now in no danger from it.

Lieutenant McIntosh and his team were incredulous, how had ZANLA got into the position to interdict them?! It was obvious it was now known that they'd escaped the encirclement. Perhaps the enemy had tried another attack or, more likely, the ZANLA they encountered on their way out had mentioned they'd seen some 'comrades' and two and two had been added together. Whatever the reason, the SAS men knew that they and their cover had been well and truly blown. The priority now was to keep moving and not give ZANLA the opportunity to contain them. The fact that the callsign had seen no enemy movement as they crossed the fields led them to believe ZANLA were communicating with each other by radio. If so, this latest contact would have already been reported and large numbers of terrorists would be rushing to the scene.

The SAS team ran, almost at the sprint, across the grassland. From their map appreciations they knew the next obstacle was a river. When they reached it, the callsign intended to plunge in then swim for the far bank.

After a while Lieutenant McIntosh considered it safe enough to stop just long enough put out a brief sitrep and call for the Lynx to join them.

The team pushed onwards. By now the callsign was running past herds of cattle and bewildered civilians. These cattle herdsman had heard the shooting and quickly realised these 'ZANLA' weren't who they appeared to be. They began to shout and point, marking the SAS's position to the terrorists. Behind them, several hundred yards away, a large group of ZANLA had appeared and were now in hot pursuit. One of the team commented that they appeared to be heavily laden, which was some consolation, insofar as they would quickly tire themselves out. Lieutenant McIntosh shouted instructions to his team and, on his command, the SAS men stopped, turned and began shooting. The terrorists scattered and threw themselves to the ground. No one was hit but the rouse served to put more distance between the callsign and ZANLA while the latter waited for the Rhodesian's to get out of rifle range.

On the callsign ran, skirting around a few kraals and cutting straight through others, harried every step of the way by civilians who were shouting and pointing them out to the pursuing ZANLA. It wasn't a blind dash; SAS men were aware of the very real threat that more ZANLA may appear in front of them so moderated their own speed to give them time to react accordingly should they run into another ambush.

The callsign stopped and put the pursuing ZANLA under fire a few more times and gained an extra fifty yards or so on each occasion. Surely the terrorists couldn't keep this pace up? By now the SAS men had been running almost non-stop for at least a couple of miles, it must be only a question of time before ZANLA fell by the wayside exhausted?

As they were running through more pasture the callsign suddenly came under fire from their front. A lone light machinegun had opened up on them from several hundred yards away. ZANLA had deployed stop groups! The distance meant the fire was inaccurate but a stray bullet would kill just as effectively as an aimed one. To add insult to injury the SAS team began to find themselves under mortar fire. The ZANLA giving chase had been seen carrying light mortars, so they must have decided to deploy them. The HE rounds were bursting long, short and wide, kicking up the earth and sending shrapnel in all directions but, amazingly, the SAS men were spared injury. It was realised that there was no way the team could outrun ZANLA, they were communicating with each other by radio and could bring in men from all over the area to cut the Rhodesian's off.

As soon as they were clear of the machinegun, Lieutenant McIntosh called another halt. The radio operator made contact with Rhodesia and told them about the situation the team now faced, in turn he was informed that a helicopter was now at the FOB and was being prepped for the rescue mission, in addition a pair of Hunter fighter-bombers were also being armed up and would be sent to support them as soon as possible. This cheered the SAS men up a little, but they'd been told that they couldn't expect any help from the Hunters for at least an hour and the rescue helicopter thirty minutes after that. In their current predicament ninety minutes was like ninety hours, but the callsign dug in to make that one final push.

After running another mile or so and coming under fire on two more occasions from ZANLA stop groups out to their front, several changes of direction saw the team in an area which afforded some cover from view. There was scrub and scattered trees, beyond which lay the river. Incredibly, the ZANLA party who had been following them all this way were still in hot pursuit. The SAS had built up a good lead but this would be eroded soon enough as they decided to use the ground to their advantage and stand and fight. According to their watches, the Lynx was due overhead in a matter of minutes. This was the time to turn the tables on the terrorists.

Getting into position on the edge of the trees, the callsign looked on as ZANLA closed. The terrorists were moving quite quickly and the SAS men could see that they had a couple of men in front who were following their spoor.

Suddenly, one of the team spotted a second group of ZANLA – approximately 100 strong – who were manoeuvring themselves into position along a ridge to the rear of the trees. More men were seen on the callsign's right flank. With the river to their left, and most likely more ZANLA on the far bank, the SAS were now well and truly cut off. Someone opined that they were outnumbered by at least fifty to one.

With the Rhodesian's boxed in, ZANLA appeared to be in no hurry to finish the fight. A probing attack was made from the front but, after a brief but extremely vicious exchange of fire, it was quickly beaten off by the SAS men. As the attackers retreated in some disarray, leaving two of their comrades dead in the dust, the SAS were treated to a display of the terrorist's combined firepower. The whole area was saturated with rifle and machinegun fire from three sides which had the callsign hugging the ground for cover. Bullets tore through the trees, ricocheting wildly in all directions and several mortar rounds exploded near to where the Rhodesian's had last been seen. Expecting to find themselves on the end of some gunfire, the callsign had changed position and were now relatively safe from the worst of the incoming fire.

Another, smaller, probing attack was launched from the ridgeline to their rear which the callsign repelled in short order. It was now obvious what the terrorists were up to; they were attempting to draw the Rhodesian's fire so they could then concentrate their own on their positions.

Not long afterwards, the SAS men got their first break. The Lynx had shown up some way east of their location and was orbiting high in the sky as it waited their instruction. The callsign's radio operator made contact and Lieutenant McIntosh took over to act as forward air controller. He passed on the location of the enemy to the Lynx crew as well as their own position (so that the pilot knew exactly where the friendly forces were in relation to the enemy, thus lessening the chances of their being shot at by mistake).

The Lynx was quickly overhead, making a pass with its machineguns blazing into the ZANLA lines to the callsign's front. It banked away, turning and climbing hard to escape the fire being put up against it. The terrorists were firing rifles, machineguns and even RPG-7s at the Lynx as it prepared to come in for a second pass. Given the volume of fire the aircraft was forced to remain at fairly high altitude for its next run in, but was still within small arms range. The Lynx then strafed the ridge, attracting even more ground fire as it did. Undeterred, the Lynx came in for a third run; given the proximity of the SAS to the enemy, they were reluctant to fire their under wing rockets, choosing instead to make another pass with machineguns.

The Lynx returned to an orbit of the scene, drawing fire from ZANLA and therefore relieving some of the pressure on the SAS men. The Rhodesian's knew that it was entirely possible that FRELIMO MiG-17s might show up to attack the little aircraft and bomb the area in which the SAS were hiding, but the prospect of having an air to air missile launched against them didn't deter the crew of the Lynx.

Before long the Lynx moved off to orbit an area south of the location. The callsign members knew what was happening and awaited the next move. Suddenly, two Hunter jet aircraft came screaming fast and low over the scene before climbing high to circle overhead. This was a first and last warning to ZANLA and everyone involved knew the terrorists would be most unwise not to take it seriously. One false move by them would see both planes swoop down to rake them with 30mm cannon fire and high explosive rockets. Although the terrorists began to shoot at the Hunters, it was ineffectual, only serving to further mark their locations to the pilots.

Both the SAS team and ZANLA knew that there was now little prospect of FRELIMO fighters entering the fray. The MiG pilots were always wary of RhAF Hunters and the sidewinder missiles they carried.

The callsign radio crackled into life to inform them that the helicopter was inbound; it would come in fast and low in to extract the SAS men. It was going to be a dangerous manoeuvre for the Alouette, as it was sure to attract much ground fire from the assembled terrorists. The chances of the chopper being shot down or made to force land were very high; if the worst happened there would be no option but to call in second machine to rescue the survivors.

One of the Hunters banked and dived earthward, putting a long burst of cannon fire into the ZANLA positions on the ridge, with large calibre, high explosive shells bursting among them, the terrorists busied themselves scrambling for cover, Just then, as the fighter was climbing away at full power, the Alouette appeared. The noise of its engine was lost momentarily beneath the scream of the Hunters own Rolls Royce Avon. For those vital few seconds' confusion reigned among the terrorists as the jet banked over hard as if to make a second pass.

The SAS team saw the Alouette making its high speed treetop approach and threw a smoke grenade to indicate their position. Without further ado the chopper came in to land. Its engine was still almost at takeoff power as the SAS team scrambled aboard and, after a 'GO!' from the chopper tec, the machine lifted off, turning as it climbed before skimming the trees on its way out. By this time it was under quite intense fire from ZANLA, but the Hunter swooped in again – holding its fire this time – making the terrorists put their heads down once more. The tec had already manned the door mounted machinegun and was hammering away at the terrorists he could see running about only forty or so feet beneath him as the chopper passed overhead.

The Alouette had broken through the ZANLA encirclement and, chased by some more fire until it was out of small arms range, began to head home….

SIX: WAR BY ANOTHER MEANS. 1977

The bush war had seen the SAS deploy by all manner of means; by vehicle, helicopter, on foot, or static-line and freefall parachute. One of the core skills of any Rhodesian SAS operator was the ability handle canoes and small boats. Rivers, sometimes fast flowing and hundreds of yards wide when swollen by the rains, were very prevalent throughout the area of SAS operations. There was also Lake Kariba, which bordered Rhodesia and Zambia, across which the SAS made frequent incursions. To the east, just inside the Mozambique border was situated the Cabora Bassa. Both bodies of water were impressive in terms of their sheer size; Lake Kariba is 139 miles long and up to 25 miles in width, with Cabora Bassa some 150 miles long by, in parts 19 miles wide. Both are deep and dark and in places plunge to depths of around 320 and 515 feet respectively.

In Mozambique, the SAS faced unique problems. While Both FRELIMO and the Zambian military were in possession of sophisticated air defence networks in the form of search and tracking radars, SAM missile batteries and more traditional AA guns, the Zambian's always seemed reluctant to use them to interdict RhAF aircraft operating without permission in their airspace for fear of retaliation from the Rhodesian's. For FRELIMO – who were virtually at war with Rhodesia – there were no such constraints. Any RhAF planes which seen on FRELIMO radar screens were fair game for the missiles and guns. There was also the ever present threat of action from the Mozambique Air Force, though they tended to steer well clear of the action for fear that RhAF Hunter fighters might be present.

With this in mind, any RhAF transport plane or helicopter which was depositing SAS troops was liable to come under attack, especially since FRELIMO had gotten into the habit of moving their smaller calibre AA weapons about the bush at random intervals. What the RhAF might have considered a safe route for a low-level penetration could easily mean by using it they could run into heavy fire.

These ongoing difficulties, encountered during both infiltration and extraction, meant the SAS began to look at alternatives in order to keep the pressure up on ZANLA and FRELIMO without the dangers faced during movements by air. There was another consideration; the RhAF was only a relatively small force with modest fixed and rotary wing capabilities. Given the challenges Rhodesia faced, militarily as well as economically, the RhAF simply couldn't afford to lose aircraft. Under other circumstances, if the RhAF had been able to resupply itself from abroad, this would not have been as much of an issue, but sanctions meant they were simply unable to replace aircraft lost to enemy action.

While deep penetration behind-the-lines operations still meant using aircraft, the SAS were confident that concentrations of enemies and their facilities along the northern banks of the Cabora Bassa could be attacked by other means.

The task of hitting ZANLA and FRELIMO was handed over to SAS Captain Robert McKenzie. His brief was simple; find a way to operate around the Cabora Bassa area and one which would allow the SAS to maintain attacks on the enemy over sustained periods of time without being compromised. *'Bob' McKenzie was an American who served as a paratrooper with the 101st Airborne during the Vietnam War, finally ending his service as a battalion commander.*

He travelled to Rhodesia in 1970 and volunteered for service with the SAS. As with all potential recruits, McKenzie had to undergo the trials and tribulations of SAS selection before being allowed to join the Squadron. Upon successfully completing the course he was sent to serve with C Squadron with the rank of Trooper (private).

His abilities soon marked him out among his fellow soldiers as well as the Squadron's leadership and he was eventually commissioned.

During his time with the SAS, he was elevated to the rank of Major and went on to command his own Squadron. He was also awarded the Silver and Bronze Cross of Rhodesia.

Pouring over the maps of the area, Captain McKenzie immediately realised that a small group of SAS could operate from the Cabora Bassa, holing up on some of the small islands which ran the length of the lake. From there they could strike with virtual impunity at targets both on the shoreline and further inland. While they stirred up a hornet's nest the enemy would be by searching the countryside for the elusive saboteurs, wasting much time and many valuable resources in the process, but would never even consider the fact that whoever was hitting them, could be coming in off the great lake.

When Captain McKenzie put his proposals to the SAS leadership they were equally enthusiastic. He was told to assemble a team of twelve men and prepare them for operations on the Cabora Bassa.

Captain McKenzie determined to emulate the 'old-fashioned' SAS tactic (used since the regiment's formation during the North African campaign of WW2) of hit and run. His team would appear from nowhere under cover of darkness to strike hard where it would hurt ZANLA most, before apparently vanishing into thin air. He was confident that the callsign would be able to inflict much grievous damage with relative impunity. Apart from direct assaults, the SAS would also make a point of laying mines on the numerous roads and tracks being used by ZANLA and FRELIMO to ferry men and equipment towards Rhodesia. The more he thought about it the more he became convinced that his little band of men would create level of mayhem out of all proportion to their small size.

Apart from the obvious, a lesser known bonus of this style of SAS activity would be to sap enemy morale. If the Rhodesian's were popping up all over the place to attack them, ZANLA and FRELIMO would quickly begin to feel unsafe in areas which were otherwise known to be secure.

Once selected, the team found themselves at Lake McIlwaine, a large manmade body of water to the south-west of the Rhodesian capital, Salisbury. It was a place well used by the SAS for boat and dive training and now the SAS team were there to carry out exhaustive refresher training and rehearsal for the forthcoming mission. Security was as tight as ever and, as a result, only Captain McKenzie knew the reason for their being there.

Their boats for this particular operation were the SAS 'Klepper' canoe; lightweight collapsible craft which were capable of carrying two men and a modest amount of equipment. They were ideal for the task ahead as they could be paddled quickly, had little noise signature and – being so low to the waterline – had virtually no silhouette; indeed, if Zambian fishermen were out on the lake at night, the Klepper's could pass by relatively closely without being seen. That same difficulty to spot would also apply to anyone looking out across the lake from the shore.

The men trained and refined their (sometimes rusty) skills as they plied their way here and there across the lake. On one occasion the weather turned, making the surface of the water extremely choppy. This was good news for Captain McKenzie as his men could expect the same conditions when operating on the Cabora Bassa. The team was out most of the day, battling across the lake and back in increasingly hostile conditions. The

Klepper's always performed well in heavy water and now was no exception. The main difference being that here the SAS had the luxury of a safety boat to get them out of trouble, when they found their way onto the Cabora Bassa they'd be on their own. If, for any reason, a Klepper floundered the men escaping it would have to hang on to another boat until they reached safety. That could mean many miles spent over several hours immersed in the cold waters of the lake. Anyone with a vivid imagination would soon get spooked at being in the water of the Cabora Bassa; apart from crocodiles, the lake was home to the Tiger Fish, a ferocious predator with massive teeth which often grew to enormous sizes. There were numerous reports of local people being attacked by these beasts and (unconfirmed or not) the thought of one sliding in beneath to water to take a lump out of you wasn't good for the nerves.

Finally, when the preparations were complete, the team was bussed to their jumping off point on the Rhodesian/Mozambique border. It was here that they were finally informed of the operation. They were to be operating on the Cabora Bassa for six weeks and during that time they'd be resupplied by parachute drop from Dakota transport planes. Given the enemy presence throughout the area between the frontline and the lake, the use of helicopters was out of the question; the noise footprint generated by a chopper would be sure to be heard by either ZANLA or FRELIMO and it would be obvious to them that the Rhodesian's were dropping off or picking up troops. The enemy would them be sure to search the area which could blow the operation even before it got started. With this in mind, the SAS would instead be infiltrating along a river which fed in to a point on the southern bank of the Cabora Bassa.

Equipment was loaded into the canoes; each item was packed into waterproof bags for safety. The men were only able to take a minimal amount of personal kit as the priority was given to the various items of ordnance needed.

For this mission they would be dressed as ZANLA and were heavily armed with a wide assortment of captured terrorist weapons, including a couple of RPG-7 launchers. Each man also carried a semi-automatic pistol in a shoulder holster, plus spare magazines and ammo; this was an unusual armament for the Rhodesian SAS operator but necessary on this job for, if any of them suddenly found themselves in the water and separated from the others, the idea was they'd still have a weapon with which to defend themselves if needs be as they carried out the long evasion to Rhodesia.

Squeezing aboard, the Klepper's were eased out from the bank and into midstream in the last few minutes of daylight. The water was fast flowing and the speed good, but it would still take the best part of a day to reach the start point for the mission proper.

It was fully dark as the little six-boat flotilla passed over the border. From here on it was the very definition of 'bandit country', ZANLA and FRELIMO were present in large numbers everywhere. Careful use of their paddles meant that the team made only the minimum amount of noise. Each man was on high alert, looking for signs of movement along the banks and waiting for a sudden challenge or gunshot. The SAS men saw the shadowy hulks of crocodiles slithering into the water from each side of the river as the beasts spotted their canoes but, thankfully, there were no two-legged predators.

A few hours into the journey the team encountered their first real obstacle; a stretch of white water which frothed and splashed angrily for several hundred yards. Although they were expecting it, the team did not realise the full ferocity of the rapids until they were swept into them. The flimsy Klepper's took a beating as they attempted to negotiate the endless rocks protruding haphazardly from the water. Several boats were damaged and one sunk (though its crew managed to escape to the shore).

Once out of the far end of the rapids, there was no alternative for Captain McKenzie but to order the team ashore. It was soon discovered that, despite the waterproof bags, most of the equipment had been soaked through in the encounter. The lost Klepper was found semi-submerged a little way downstream after being spat out by the turbulent water. It was recovered and brought onto dry land.

Captain McKenzie knew that his team could go no further in their present state, so ordered them to make camp. Withdrawing into the undergrowth out of range of any marauding crocodiles, a situation report was passed to SAS HQ before the team settled down to rest until the sun came up.

The following morning the team set about repairing the damaged Klepper's. It was a scorching hot day and laying their kit out meant it dried rapidly in the heat.

By the time darkness fell, the SAS were ready to recommence their journey.

From here on in, the river slowed and widened until it emptied itself into the southern edge of the Cabora Bassa. Pushing off into the water, the team quickly assembled themselves in single file formation and began to paddle cautiously downstream.

They had been travelling without further incident for a couple of hours when an arm signal from the lead Klepper brought the others to a halt. There, mid-channel was an enormous bull hippopotamus. The leviathan had seen the canoes as they approached and was on high alert. For their part, the SAS men knew how to read the body language of this mighty beast and realised it was preparing to defend its territory.

The hippopotamus may seem like a docile, even comical, creature to those who know no different but for others with the correct knowledge it is a deadly adversary; in fact it is far more dangerous than any big cat as far as humans are concerned. Ill tempered and unstoppable, each year hippos continue to kill hundreds of people in Africa.

The slightest wrong move would have seen the hippo charge and wreak carnages among the flotilla. It had planted itself sentinel-like and was not going to give an inch of ground. There was absolutely no way the team could hope to sail past it, for a start the river was too narrow and even had it not been, it was obvious from the hippo's posture that it would never let them pass anyway.

Back paddling cautiously away from the immediate threat, the boats made for the bank. Captain McKenzie announced there was no alternative but to carry the boats and everything in them across land to a point where they would be clear of the threat.

Making sure they gave the beast as wide a berth as possible lest it suddenly decided to come ashore and chase them (a hippo can run much faster than a man over short distances), the team began to manhandle the Klepper's though the undergrowth. It was a physically demanding and time consuming task, but they were eventually able to re-launch the boats further down river.

Some hours later, while it was still dark, they arrived at the mouth of the river. There, to their front, lay the mighty Cabora Bassa. In between them and it was an incredibly dense area of reeds which they would have to negotiate before they could break out onto the lake. Once they got in amongst the reeds the enormity of the obstacle became apparent as they became enveloped to a point where they could not see the other boats. Immediately the nature of the reed beds began to slow them down to a crawl. The reeds were tall and orientation quickly became another issue but, after much hard toil, the Klepper's were eventually nosed through to the far side.

At last the SAS men found themselves on the dark

waters of the great lake. What should have a single night's journey had turned into two. It had been like a remake of 'The African Queen'!

Fate had not yet finished with the team. A stiff headwind was blowing across the water as they struck out in search of their first LUP, and as a result their progress was stifled even further.

It was with little time to spare that the team made 'landfall'. The land was actually a patch of foul smelling mud jutting out of the water only a matter of inches above the waterline. There were a few sorry looking trees dotted about, but little more. It was far from ideal but, as the sun was now peeping over the distant hills, it would have to do. The Klepper's were dragged into cover over the shin deep gloop, camouflage nets and bivvies erected to hide the team and provide some shade from the blazing sun and, after all routines had been observed, the men were allowed to rest.

The following night the SAS men moved to another more suitable position where they could set up their first FOB. This little island was ideal for the first phase of the operation; close enough to the initial targets to be within easy canoe range and remote enough to make sure the enemy should never come looking.

During the early hours of the next night an RhAF Dakota came in low over the lake, guided in by radio by the SAS, it para-dropped several containers full of landmines, ammunition and other supplies – including a fresh meal for the men on the ground. Knowing that it would have been spotted as it came in over Cabora Bassa, either by radar or eyes on the ground, the Dakota flew straight and level for almost the full length of the lake before turning towards Rhodesia then dropping a few soccer ball sized 'Alpha' anti-personnel bombs on the location of a suspected ZANLA holding base. It was simply a case of the dispatcher throwing the bombs through the open door, when they hit the dirt they'd bounce to about head height before exploding and showering the area with metal fragments. The ploy was simple; to make the enemy believe that the plane had been on a bombing mission and not a delivery run.

As darkness fell on the third day it was time for the SAS to go into action. A four-man callsign set out to lay anti-tank landmines on a known ZANLA infiltration route. The target road was a dirt track affair, typical of the area, and it lay about five miles from the shoreline in an area which ZANLA was sure was safe from Rhodesian predation.

Extra care was taken on the approach; the callsign was determined not to leave any spoor in their wake. To this end they elected to travel barefoot while adhering to the usual anti-tracking measures.

Once at the target area the men carefully picked out the tracks which were most obviously in use by ZANLA vehicles. To give the best chance of success, it wasn't simply a case of placing the mines on the surface of the tracks then hoping for the best, each mine would be placed under the surface in ruts which vehicles had made by running through over long periods of time. The first step was to remove the top soil onto a small canvas sheet, the earth below was then placed into a sandbag. After the mine was laid, and the fuse and anti-handling device set, the top soil would be replaced to disguise the device from view. Great care was taken to blend in the earth so that it matched its surroundings and no sign of disturbance could be seen. Afterwards the sandbag of soil was taken away and scattered where it wouldn't be found.

In all, eight anti-tank mines were seeded throughout the immediate vicinity before the callsign returned to the lake.

Arriving back at the FOB the patrol as a whole made a move to another location. The equipment dropped to them had been carefully buried and this island was now to become a supply dump for the duration of the operation. Whenever supplies of ammunition, landmines or explosives were required, the team could return to draw them.

The team found another place to rest about five miles away from their new supply dump. This was another inhospitable place, thick with putrid smelling mud and home to billions of flies. When the sun rose the heat rapidly became almost unbearable. Later on that same day, during the scheduled radio report, some good news was passed to the SAS team. According to intercepted radio traffic, it was confirmed that a vehicle had ran over one of the landmines. There were several fatalities, including a senior FRELIMO officer. It was a good start for all involved. Killing a high-ranking Freddie could only ever have been dreamed of but, with their very first attempt, they'd bagged a 'star prize'.

Traffic had been brought to a halt while FRELIMO swept the trails in the vicinity for mines. They had access to a few Russian made mine detectors to make this task easier but, unless they placed some explosives on the mines and blew them up in situ, Freddie would be forced to attempt to defuse the devices. The SAS had made sure each one was fitted with an anti-handling device. Any disturbance, however minor, as the mine was being dealt with and it would explode, taking the EOD man and anyone in close proximity with it.

The report also said that FRELIMO were mounting a large-scale operation to find the Rhodesian saboteurs responsible, their lack of security while passing radio messages to each other were giving the intelligence people the heads up as to the nature of the search.

Not wishing to rest on their laurels, Captain McKenzie and his team decided to go back into action as soon as the hullabaloo had died down.

A target had already been selected; a main road running

between two towns which the SAS knew from their intelligence reports of the area was a major line of communication for both FRELIMO and ZANLA.

A couple of nights later the team struck out for a point on the banks of the Cabora Bassa from which they could strike out for the target. Pulling the Klepper's under cover then camouflaging them and leaving a couple of men behind as guards, the rest of the team made their way inland.

The target road was not close to the shoreline and this suited the SAS. To keep hitting targets immediately around and about the vicinity of the lake may well make pennies drop. Their best defence was the fact that both FRELIMO and ZANLA would never suspect there was a team of Rhodesian SF operating on the Cabora Bassa.

The SAS moved through the bush, it was hard going all the way through dense scrub. Finally, they arrived at the road. The 'highway' was in poor shape; even by African standards, deeply rutted and peppered with cavernous potholes. This was good news for the team as, this time they weren't going to lay mines, but carry out an ambush. They knew that to suddenly have Rhodesian soldiers appearing here in the back of beyond would have a deep psychological impact on anyone using the road for weeks, if not months, to come.

The SAS were aware that the road was in use at all times of the day and night, so the only thing to do was to select a suitable ambush point then settle down to wait for the first worthwhile target.

The team had been in position for a couple of hours when what appeared to be a truck came bouncing into view a few hundred yards away. Captain McKenzie got the night vision scope on it and identified it as a Land Rover. The road conditions were such that the vehicle couldn't travel much beyond jogging speed, which gave the ambush party plenty of time to ready themselves. The signal was simple. The contact would be initiated by Captain McKenzie himself and, upon hearing gunfire, the rest of the men would join in.

Captain McKenzie got the vehicle in his sights then – when it closed to the optimum point – let fly with his rifle. Suddenly the air erupted with gunfire and the Land Rover swerved and skidded into to brush opposite. The shooting continued for a few seconds then all was still. There was no movement from the vehicle. Some men went forward to investigate. They found a few bodies on the ground then, inside the vehicle, more dead and dying.

The SAS counted ten in total including three men on the front bench seat. They were wearing FRELIMO uniforms and carrying rifles.

Those still alive quickly expired and the SAS set to work pulling them clear of the vehicle then checking them and the Land Rover for items of intelligence value. The FRELIMO men were relieved of their ammunition and the bolts taken from their rifles (to be dumped in the lake later on) before the guns were thrown back in inside. The Land Rover was then set on fire and the SAS team withdrew.

They cut south-west for a while, away from the lake so as to draw attention to possible hiding places in the opposite direction to Cabora Bassa. There was little anti-tracking and this was done for a purpose. Several hundred yards into the move Captain McKenzie instructed one of the men to booby-trap the trail in the hope of killing a few FRELIMO during their follow-up operation and deterring others from trying to track them.

After following a long and circuitous route, diligently anti-tracking the rest of the way, the SAS found themselves back at the lake.

A couple of days later Captain McKenzie decided to take his team across the Cabora Bassa to try their luck against targets they knew were available to them along a portion of its northern bank. They returned to the arms dump to stock up on munitions before making the move and, as a result, the Klepper's were very heavily laden and sitting even lower in the water than usual.

After several hours of hard paddling, the team made landfall on a small scrap of land protruding out of the water a few hundred yards from the shore. In stark contrast to where they'd been spending their time this little island was paradise. Although it was still interminably hot, this new LUP wasn't the sea of putrid mud like the others they'd been forced to endure.

Captain McKenzie had chosen the new LUP carefully; it was within striking distance of a small FRELIMO base to which he decided he and his team should pay a visit. The Captain had all the necessary intelligence on the place to mount a successful night-time attack.

Later that day he briefed the men as to the forthcoming operation and they began their preparations accordingly.

That evening, shortly after last light, the twelve men set out, paddling carefully towards the shore and making landfall within an area where it was easy to conceal the Klepper's. They were confident they hadn't been seen on the approach, but the vicinity was swept with the night vision scope just to make sure no one was lurking unseen in the darkness. Retrieving their weaponry from the boats, they set off into the night.

It was tough going. The undergrowth was incredibly dense in places and conspired to slow the progress to little more than a crawl but, eventually, they came upon the dirt road which would lead them all the way to the target. Intelligence reports indicated that the road was only used during daylight hours, and then infrequently. It had been raining so Captain McKenzie got one of the men to dig down into one of the puddles which had formed in the tyre ruts and place an anti-tank mine. The rains were set continue over the coming hours so it was almost a certainty that, when the FRELIMO reaction force responded to the news of the attack, the mine would still be submerged and undetectable. The first vehicle to pass along the road – and everyone in it – would be blown to kingdom come.

The raiding party eventually closed on the target. The FRELIMO base was a small affair; a few brick built buildings lined up along the edge of a makeshift airstrip. Captain McKenzie and a couple of others crept forward to make an appreciation of the place through the NV scope. There was no sign of life outside and, helpfully, no sentries. Here, deep inside Mozambique, those manning the camp were confident they were too far away from the war to let the prospect of attack bother them. The lights were on in several of the buildings and music from a radio could be heard drifting through the darkness. The only other sound was the thump of a diesel generator. Captain McKenzie's intelligence report told him that there could be up to forty FRELIMO ensconced at the base at any one time and his own appraisal of the situation led him to concur.

The recce party withdrew and a plan was quickly formulated. The raiding party would split into three four-man groups, each one being responsible for hitting the three occupied buildings. The attack would take place at close range (sub-100 yards) and the raiders would put as much fire down on the target as possible in the time frame allowed.

By the time the SAS had gotten into position the generator had been switched off. There were now no lights shining from the uncurtained windows, indicating that the garrison members had retired to bed. The cue for the attack to commence was one of Captain McKenzie's party firing an RPG-7 HE round.

As the men watched on in the darkness, the RPG gunner took aim. It was time to give FRELIMO a rude awakening. The round struck its target with a satisfying flash and bang just as the night erupted in gunfire. Several more RPG rockets were fired into all three buildings as the SAS gunners got them in their sights. The buildings were made from mud bricks with tin roofs and as such were not up to the task of withstanding high-velocity rifle fire. The bullets passed straight through into the interior to cause havoc amongst those inside.

After ninety-seconds silence fell over the scene. There had been no attempt to break out of the buildings and no return fire. As the others looked on, four men dashed forwards to throw fragmentation and phosphorous grenades into each building before 'killing' the generator with another frag.

It was now time to depart. There was a village only a stone's throw from the base and the SAS expected some kind of reaction from it. They cleared the field and cut away into the bush until they came across a game trail which ran north to south towards the lake. It was virtually impossible to leave sign on these trails; trampled as they were to a concrete like hardness by decades of use by countless millions of hooves.

The SAS men made good time and the five miles back to the Cabora Bassa was done at almost a run all the way. The team knew they were now to the east of where the Klepper's had been hidden, so decided to cut along the shoreline. Wary of the ever present crocodile threat, they began to thread their way over numerous obstacles which lay between them and the boats. Fallen trees, exposed roots and half a hundred other hazards made for exceedingly slow progress; indeed, such was the difficulty of the terrain that it took several hours to navigate their way the mile from the start point to where the boats were cached. The SAS men were exhausted as they put their kit aboard and squashed themselves in among it. They set off for the island LUP, arriving behind schedule and just as the sun was coming up.

It had been a good night for the SAS. They'd managed to get the drop on a sizable number of FRELIMO where they – FRELIMO – thought they were safe. Again, the ramifications of the attack would reverberate far and wide, sapping the morale of others as they realised that they too were could suddenly find themselves victims of the phantom squads of Rhodesian's they were now convinced were hiding out in the bush.

During the early morning the sound of a distant explosion rolled out across the water. The SAS men knew that their hidden landmine had been triggered. FRELIMO had just lost another vehicle and some more men. It was raining and the heat and humidity was unbearable, but the men were cheered at their success.

That same night a Dakota came in to carry out a resupply mission. The rain had cleared enough to allow the plane to fly. It came in slow and extremely low, dropping each of the containers bang on target into the centre of the little island. As before, on it flew, to make a diversionary attack with Alpha bombs on some distant FRELIMO target before turning for Rhodesia. Among the ammunition, fresh batteries and other stores, came cigarettes and gas canisters for the tiny camping stoves the SAS had carried all the way from home. Now, instead of 'hard routine' they were able to prepare some much welcomed hot food.

A radio report from Rhodesia informed the SAS men that intercepted messages said that FRELIMO had turned out in force to hunt for them and were combing the whole area. They appeared to have no clue how the Rhodesian's were moving or where they were, but assumed they were somewhere on land. A watch was put on the shoreline but no enemy activity was spotted.

After laying low the following day, Captain McKenzie decided to change location again, moving further east along the lake in search of more trade. The Klepper's were loaded with as much as they could carry and the rest of the stores buried for later use.

It was to be a long voyage so the little flotilla set off not land after last light. Not far into the move a storm blew up from nowhere, lashing the lake and whipping up large waves. The ferocity of the squall was such that it's like had never been experienced by the canoeists. They soon found themselves forced to run for the cover of the shoreline but, even there the conditions were such that they were having great difficulty controlling the Klepper's. They paddled onwards for another half mile or so until it became apparent that they could go no further.

The boats were beached and dragged out of harm's way into the undergrowth then the men settled down into their makeshift camp. They were waiting for a break in the weather so they could continue the journey eastwards, but the storm had other ideas.

In the early hours of the following morning, the wind and rain had abated just enough to make launching the Klepper's feasible. With the attempt to find a new base now postponed, the team would return to their FOB and decide on a new course of action once there. The six canoes were returned to the water and the SAS men paddled them back 'home'. This time, with the wind at their backs, the progress was swift and the SAS made it back to their little island in the half light of the new day.

After resting up then making a full appreciation of other targets available to him within the area, Captain McKenzie decided that they might be able to salvage something out of the previous night's fiasco. He instructed one of his senior NCOs to lead a six-man callsign on a mission to place landmines along a known main ZANLA supply route. The team was briefed and began their preparations. From the southern shore to the target road would take some hours of hard slog for the heavily laden SAS men and, combined with the actual minelaying and return journey, it would be daylight by the time they returned to the lake. With travelling by day on the water out of the question (there were fishermen aplenty all over the lake who would quickly report any suspicious activity, especially if they saw an unfamiliar craft like the Klepper). The callsign would have to go to ground and wait out the daylight hours in the hope that the inevitable ZANLA and FRELIMO reaction did not extend as far as the shoreline.

After last light the callsign set off. The wind had eased by now and the lake had returned to some semblance of normality. From their position – a narrow part of the lake – it was quite reasonable to strike out for the southern shore. The callsign made landfall without incident and, after collapsing then hiding the canoes, set off towards the target.

It took more than nine hours to reach the road, the terrain had been terribly unforgiving every step of the way with thick – almost impassable – vicious Jesse thorn bushes continually barring their passage. Everyone was suffering from cuts and bruises as they finally settled down into cover within visual range of the target. According to the plan they should have been back at the water's edge by now, but there was nothing else to do but stay here for the rest of the day to watch and wait. They made contact with the main force back on the island and informed them of the difficulties and that their return would be delayed accordingly as a result. Not long after daybreak traffic began to build up on the road. Heavy vehicles belonging to both ZANLA and FRELIMO were moving in both directions. It was obvious that, once laid, the mines would soon be struck.

The callsign waited until well after the last vehicle of the day passed before moving forward to the track. With two men on lookout duties, the others began the task of laying the mines. As described previously, the SAS were always most careful to hide the fact that landmines were present from prying eyes. The points in which they were to be laid were always carefully considered and they were each meticulously placed, using top soil to blend them back in with the surrounding earth. When placed in tyre ruts, the earth would be sculpted back into shape so that no disturbance could be seen and, on this occasion, because it had been raining, the SAS men took time out to flick water from their canteens across the site of the mines to emulate the action of raindrops on the soil.

As they withdrew, the SAS came upon a game trail along which they were able to pass towards the lake. Much time and effort was saved and the team were able to make up enough time that they were able to take to the water and paddle back to the LUP before sun up.

The next mission was another attack upon a road used by ZANLA and FRELIMO to move men and materials towards Rhodesia's northern border with Mozambique. The whole team was to undertake this operation and, after making the crossing to the southern shoreline where the boats were hidden and a couple of men left to stand guard. Captain McKenzie led the others away from the lake, in a southerly direction, for about six miles. The going was hard, but not as difficult as that faced by the mine laying party a couple of nights previous.

Once at the road the SAS selected a suitable point to lay a mine. The usual procedures were observed and the result was a mine which was so perfectly hidden, the SAS had to push a small stick into the ground by the track to mark its location so they knew when to expect the explosion. Instead of simply letting the landmine do the work, Captain McKenzie wanted to follow the explosion up by mounting an ambush. Perhaps there might be more than one vehicle involved in the coming incident and the opportunity to shoot up those following on behind was too tempting a prospect to pass over.

Night turned into day and as the hours passed, the expected enemy vehicles didn't materialise. Just when the ambush party thought they were onto a lemon, a tractor chugged into view. It was towing a long agricultural trailer on which were a dozen or so FRELIMO. The trailer was also piled high with stores. It was also noted that the driver was wearing FRELIMO uniform. The SAS men lay low in cover in expectation of the coming explosion but, amazingly both the tractor and trailer missed the landmine. Captain McKenzie knew he couldn't let this target pass. His shooting was the cue for the rest of his team to join in and together they quickly raked the tractor and trailer with gunfire. Those on the back had no chance and were cut down before they could respond. The driver fared no better, killed in the opening volley, he slumped in his seat as the tractor rumbled on out of control. By the time the SAS got to it, the tractor had shuddered to a stall. All the FRELIMO were dead and while some of the ambush team began to search them for documentation of items of intelligence value, Captain McKenzie clambered onto the trailer and realised just what they'd come across. The trailer was packed with rations, brand new uniforms, webbing, boots, rifles, ammunition, RPG-7 launchers and rockets, anti-tank and anti-personnel mines, mortar bombs and even a Russian made mine detector; it was a veritable treasure trove of equipment whose loss would have a serious material effect further along the FRELIMO line.

The SAS had no time to waste; although they were in a remote area they'd made a hell of a lot of noise and someone, somewhere was bound to have heard it. Ammunition was taken from the trailer and magazines recharged, the team also plundered the boxes of military rations (abandoned by the Portuguese during their withdrawal) in search of some variation to the monotony of they own diet. Both the trailer and tractor were rigged for demolition and, as the SAS withdrew, slow burning fuses were initiated. Not long afterwards, as the ambush party were working their way carefully towards the Cabora Bassa, they heard explosions. The valuable FRELIMO equipment and a vital means of transport had been destroyed.

The SAS made it back to the island safely. The following day they were informed that Rhodesian signals intercepts people had picked up a lot of radio traffic. It appeared that FRELIMO had gone into a blue funk at the loss of its men and much needed equipment.

As an aside, the landmine the SAS planted remained hidden and undisturbed until FRELIMO brought another tractor and trailer in to recover the bodies. The driver was assured that the trail was clear of landmines (after all the stricken tractor had passed over that same road); FRELIMO had swept the trail (but only by eye) just in case, satisfying themselves that all was well. The tractor missed the hidden mine but the trailer hit it, blowing it to smithereens, killing the driver and several FRELIMO who were standing close by.

It was now time for the SAS to return home. They'd been on operations on the lake for six weeks and every hour of it had proved tough; from the heat and the flies, to the storms and the harsh terrain surrounding Cabora Bassa. Each man had suffered as a result.

Despite the unforgiving nature of the reality of living and fighting in this environment, the SAS had proved the concept. Overall, the operation had been a great success. They had wrought death and destruction among the enemy and – more importantly – got FRELIMO in such a panic that they were tying up troops which otherwise would be deployed against Rhodesia or its ally, the Mozambique National Resistance (MNR) movement, to protect sites which they now knew to be vulnerable to attack.

The SAS team paddled to the south-western shoreline under cover of the darkness and made their preparations to leave Mozambique. They cleared a HLZ within the scrub and collapsed the Klepper's before calling the chopper in to extract them. The RhAF Alouettes arrived on schedule and the men boarded for the short flight over the Rhodesian border.

Back at base, they handed over the documents they had taken from the dead FRELIMO. Unbeknown to anyone at the time, one of the dead from the tractor ambush turned out to be a senior FRELIMO officer and he'd been carrying the new signal codes and frequencies for the whole Tete province. Courtesy of the SAS, the Rhodesian signals intelligence people now had the means to read encoded FRELIMO radio traffic in real time; in fact they were soon decoding messages faster than the enemy signallers.

Back at Cranborne, Captain McKenzie was extensively debriefed by C Squadron planners. The after action reports of each man and the patrol diary had already been examined to see if there was any further merit in mounting similar operations.

The verdict was unanimous; the notion of placing small groups of men on the Cabora Bassa was both militarily viable and very productive.

Before long another operation was mounted and this one caused even more havoc than the first. The lessons learned by the men on the 'proving mission' were passed on to the others and it made them all the more effective for it. They also had access to the two readymade supply dumps left behind by the original group which meant the need for aerial resupply and the risks it entailed was minimised.

A third mission saw the SAS score their biggest success

of the Cabora Bassa 'campaign', when, under cover of darkness, the team involved sneaked into the largest harbour on the lake, at the very eastern tip of the Cabora Bassa, and destroyed twenty-one FRELIMO patrol boats which were tied up at the dockside. Entering the mouth of the harbour unseen, the SAS pulled the Klepper's alongside each target; placing explosive charges under the waterline of the vessels guaranteed they sank quickly. As they withdrew out onto the lake, the SAS stopped to watch their handiwork as the delayed action explosives went up. Some of the boats fuel tanks caught fire and pools of burning petrol and diesel spilled out across the surface of the harbour, illuminating the scene for hundreds of yards. In one fell swoop, the SAS had virtually eliminated FRELIMOs ability to patrol the lake. They were unable to make up the losses so, apart from the occasional foray aboard a civilian boat, Freddie was kept off the Cabora Bassa.

Despite all the attacks, and especially the one on the harbour, FRELIMO and ZANLA never tumbled to the fact that the SAS were using the lake as a means of transporting themselves around the region. They continued to believe that small squads of men were hiding out in the bush and expended much time and effort in a vain attempt to find them.

SEVEN: INTO THE CAULDRON. 1977

The SAS had been operating in Mozambique for eight years, during that time they'd wreaked untold damage on both the FRELIMO and ZANLA war machines. As the war escalated, the Rhodesian high command wished to expand that success to cover parts of the country which, up to that point, had received relatively little attention from C Squadron.

During their time in the Tete province, the SAS had slowly wrested control of the communications network away from FRELIMO. It was no exaggeration to say that the enemy could now not safely travel along any road or trail without the prospect of running into SAS ambushes or hidden landmines. As a result the FRELIMO and ZANLA logistics chains had virtually collapsed, causing widespread difficulties for their operations into Rhodesia throughout that sector and reducing ZANLA border incursions from involving around 800 men each month to approximately 200.

Now, and with one eye on what the SAS had done in Tete, they were to be deployed into the Gaza province to find and kill as many ZANLA and FRELIMO as possible and harass their lines of communications.

The planned operations were to be on such a scale that there was no alternative but to withdraw the SAS from operations in Tete until further notice (although SAS attacks against specific ZANLA and FRELIMO would continue). Also, and to make up the numbers required, TF (Territorial Force; part-time reservists) were to be called to the colours to take part. The TF troops were SAS men who had finished their regular military engagements but were obliged to undertake periods of active service with C Squadron.

Even bolstered by its TF operators, C Squadron didn't have enough men available to do what was expected of them.

The SAS went into action in the Gaza province with a literal bang. They (alongside the RLI in most cases) mounted large-scale attacks on ZANLA camps, killing many hundreds of terrorists in the process while displacing countless more. In response to the continuing Rhodesian incursions into Gaza, FRELIMO had committed a large number of men into the province with the intention of stopping the Rhodesian's in their tracks. FRELIMO had become very aggressive and were actively seeking to engage the RSF (Rhodesian Security Forces) wherever they could be found. Large numbers of anti-aircraft units were also deployed and they soon set about making life difficult for RhAF planes.

For their part the Rhodesian's didn't let the tactical grass grow, they were constantly evolving their protocols in order to keep one step ahead of a numerically superior enemy and make the most of their own meagre resources.

One innovation was the 'fire brigade' role, where troops would respond to information from the intelligence people to make quick, pin-point raids to take out specific targets of opportunity. The beauty of this strategy was that boots could be put on the ground where they would do most damage and, once the specified target had been destroyed, the troops could be rapidly uplifted before FRELIMO could intervene.

A brief diversion: Rhodesian signals intelligence was highly sophisticated. As touched upon previously, they were reading ZANLA and FRELIMO radio traffic on a continual basis. Despite the use of ciphers – which were changed at regular intervals – it never took the intelligence people long to break into the new codes. It was a quiet contribution to the war effort, played out in backrooms by men and women who never got the recognition they deserved. As a result of their efforts much valuable information was read, collated and passed on to the relevant parties and often (as described shortly) this would translate into direct action.

The Rhodesian's were also intercepting and decoding ZIPRA and Zambian military signals with the same level of success.

For their part, Both FRELIMO and the Zambian authorities did their best to read at least some of the prolific radio output of the Rhodesian Security Forces but were unsuccessful for a variety of reasons – not just because the RSF was 'security aware' and used sophisticated codes for both Morse and voice transmissions which were changed with obsessive regularity – but they just didn't have the talent available to them to turn their efforts into results.

There was a persistent rumour that the Soviets were keen to help their ZIPRA protégées by providing the means to break and read Rhodesian signals. To this end (so the rumour went) they'd stationed a spy ship off the coast of Tanzania whose task was to intercept Rhodesian radio messages.

When FRELIMO came into the possession of advanced Chinese made signals equipment, the Rhodesian ability to decode their messages was suddenly lost. The resulting gaps in intelligence was enough to have the SAS sent in to destroy one of these new signals stations and force FRELIMO back into using their old, insecure, methods of communications.

One such Rhodesian intercept revealed that a ZANLA supply convoy was due to transport materials from the docks at Maputo to a shared FRELIMO/ZANLA holding camp and thereafter take senior ZANLA commanders and men to FOBs in the west of the country, close the Rhodesian border.

This particular intercept piqued the interest of the intelligence people because of the fact that the convoy was a ZANLA effort. Usually, the terrorists would take advantage of FRELIMOs goodwill to distribute men and materials on their behalf. FRELIMO was always eager to help and put its own logistics network at the terrorist's disposal on numerous occasions. Another reason for ZANLA wishing to attach themselves to FRELIMO columns was the fact that, even at this stage in the war, the Rhodesian government was reluctant to allow full scale attacks on FRELIMO. International opinion and the faint prospect that, perhaps, the west might come to their senses and see what Russia and China were up to (remember this was at the height of the cold war) and ease up on sanctions accordingly meant that RSF hands were often tied by the politicians.

Up until now, ZANLA simply didn't possess the capability to move enough supplies to the front in enough quantity to service the needs of the men who were encamped there, let alone equip and reinforce its Rhodesian bound gangs.

Now, it appeared that things were changing. ZANLA had found itself in possession of a fleet of brand new Chinese made trucks, supplied direct from the manufacturer courtesy of Beijing. It was a worrying development for the Rhodesian's, as it if meant the terrorists could increase their logistical efforts, they'd be able to push more of the men they had waiting in western Mozambique across the border into Rhodesia.

The formation of this new ZANLA supply column and the ramifications of it meant that the Rhodesian's wanted to see it smashed before it could be put into effect.

The signals intelligence people were aware that the

convoy was due to leave Maputo. Unwittingly the enemy had been most kind insofar as they had provided times and routes. There was no time to waste; an order was given to the SAS.

At an FOB close to the Mozambique border, a fifteen-strong SAS detachment led by Captain Colin Willis had arrived for a rapid deployment to interdict and destroy the convoy.

Captain Willis was another legendary SAS figure. He'd been born in Northern Rhodesia (Zambia). He remained in Zambia after it was granted independence until – for a prank – he painted a moustache on a poster of the President, Kenneth Kaunda. He was arrested and held in custody for a month before being expelled. The Zambian's declared that he was a political undesirable and, if he returned, he could expect a long prison sentence.

He moved to Rhodesia and decided to join the army. He served as an infantryman before electing to try his hand at the SAS selection course. After passing, Captain (then Trooper) Willis served for a while before applying for a commission. He was unable to stay with the SAS because there were no openings for officers available. Instead he left C Squadron and underwent officer training at Gwelo. Thereafter he served with the RLI for four years (being awarded a Bronze Cross of Rhodesia) before re-applying for the SAS. Captain Willis went back into Zambia on many occasions – though always as part of the RSF and took part in some of the SAS' most notable operations.

Such was his outstanding contribution to the SAS that he was awarded to coveted 'Wings on Chest' award (all operators wore their parachute wings on the top of the right sleeve). When the Rhodesian SAS were looking for a way to honour its bravest and best men, they decided that the entitlement to wear the wings, pilot fashion, on the left chest would be a suitable and distinct badge of prestige. Of all the accolades available to any SAS operator, none was more coveted than the Wings on Chest. Only a handful of men were ever given the privilege, and the extreme difficulty in earning that right marked them out as 'an SAS man among SAS men'.

Captain Willis and his team already knew the details of their mission; they were to ambush the convoy as it made its way to the FOBs – when it was full of ZANLA. It was a golden opportunity to strike at the terrorists which couldn't be missed.

The SAS team didn't have to wait long before their deployment 'over the fence' into Mozambique. They boarded a Dakota which was to take them to a DZ from where they could strike out towards the road along which the intelligence people assured them the target convoy would be travelling.

They were to be delivered by static-line parachute and, given the proliferation of FRELIMO AA assets throughout the area as well as the electronic eye of their search and tracking radars, the drop would be made at very low level, so low in fact that it was considered pointless to wear reserve parachutes. If the main 'chute failed there'd be simply no time to deploy the reserve; especially given the fact that the men would be falling faster than usual, dragged earthward by their heavy equipment loads.

Darkness had settled in before the Dakota crossed the border. It had already been zigzagging in a seemingly random pattern to confuse the watching FRELIMO radar operators. Once over enemy territory the all too real prospect of being suddenly engaged by hidden and hitherto unknown AA gun positions became a reality and the Dakota took the appropriate evasive measures to lessen the chances of it being engaged. FRELIMO gunners were very aggressive when it came to taking on the RhAF and for a large, slow flying aircraft like the Dakota, the dangers were magnified. Also, unlike a jet powered plane, the propeller driven Dakota would announce its arrival, giving FRELIMO the opportunity to prepare themselves.

Fortunately, the Dakota made it to the DZ without incident, finding its way using good old fashioned navigation skills (RhAF aircraft of this type weren't equipped with the electronic aids which were found in other aircraft). The SAS were stood to and dispatched quickly into the night sky. The men came down in a tight stick and no injuries were suffered. As they gathered up their 'chutes then prepared for the off, the Dakota probed further into the interior of the country, still carrying out its evasive manoeuvres.

When it came time to turn for home, the crew were going to employ the old Alpha bomb trick over a couple of known small ZANLA outposts.

A little later on, after the dispatchers had divested themselves of their stock of bombs, the plane settled down for the return journey. Suddenly, it was bracketed by a hail of cannon and heavy machinegun fire. The shooting was deadly accurate and the Dakota was hit by 23mm shells, 12.7mm rounds as well as small arms fire.

A brilliant piece of evasive flying by the Dakota's pilot saw his aircraft saved from certain destruction.

The plane had taken a beating in the contact, being hit numerous times, with a 23mm shell striking the cockpit and destroying some of the instrumentation. The port engine had also been hit but although running rough, was still providing power.

All aboard had escaped injury and while the Dakota was wounded, she was flyable. Force landing or bailing out here would have seen the crew in the midst of a vengeful enemy. It was odds on that they'd be quickly caught. That being the case, what happened next would be anyone's guess. They might have survived to find themselves languishing in a Mozambique prison or, perhaps more likely, they'd be beaten to death at the scene.

Exercising considerable skill, the pilot managed to coax the Dakota over the border and into friendly territory to make a successful landing at the closest FAF.

Examining the damage, it was quite clear that, had the attack come while the SAS were still aboard there would have been casualties, and most likely deaths, among them. It was a sobering thought and a lesson for all concerned that FRELIMO really did mean business.

Meanwhile, unaware of the drama surrounding the Dakota, Captain Willis and his callsign were making their way through the darkness towards the target road some nine miles away.

They arrived unseen before first light and began the process of finding a suitable place and setting themselves up in their ambush positions in anticipation of the convoy's arrival. The planners had given the SAS plenty of time to select and set up the ambush as the ZANLA supply trucks weren't due to pass for another two days.

The area was remote, remote enough for the SAS to chance placing an anti-tank mine in the road in daylight.

During the early evening, when everyone was confident there was no passing traffic to disturb them, Captain Willis ordered a mine to be laid. Breaking cover, two men set to work placing the mine while a couple of protection parties gave cover.

The team hadn't been at work long when one of the protection groups saw three men approaching along the road. They were quickly identified as being a ZANLA terrorist and two FRELIMO, what they were doing there was anyone's guess, but it was suspected they may have been sweeping the dirt road in search of hidden landmines prior to the arrival of the convoy. The three men spotted the SAS mine layer's before the protection team had chance to give warning and went for their weapons. The protection team were forced to open fire and a brief exchange of gunfire ensued. The enemy had scattered into the brush at the roadside but, instead of withdrawing to raise the alarm, they appeared to want to make a fight of it. Soon all three had been cut down.

Captain Willis now faced a dilemma. He had no idea where these men had come from and his intelligence reports had made no mention of any terrorist or FRELIMO activity in the area of the ambush site. He had to assume that these three men weren't alone (there was no reason to expect they were anyway). The gunfire carried a long way and most likely reached the ears of these men's comrades. That being the case, they'd be moving in to investigate.

The SAS had to put distance between themselves and any reaction. Time was of the essence as was the necessity to anti-track. The callsign members were well aware of the enemy's ability to follow up spoor so Captain Willis made the decision to withdraw along the road. The disadvantage of course was the SAS would be in open ground where they could be seen but, in this particular instance, the ability to move quickly over ground which had been hardened by traffic meant they'd be out of the immediate vicinity before the enemy arrived and they'd be very difficult to track.

The bodies were dragged out of cover and into the middle of the road where they could be seen. They were all booby trapped with fragmentation grenades fitted with instantaneous fuses. As soon as their ZANLA/FRELIMO comrades turned up and attempted to recover their comrades they'd detonate the grenades, anyone standing within ten yards would almost certainly be killed. A lot of people reading this would consider that a 'dirty trick', but it was one used by both sides.

The SAS team set off, moving tactically but rapidly, making sure their footfalls remained well within the hardened areas of the road. As well as the booby trapped bodies, they had left behind the mine; disguising it with the usual thoroughness until it was rendered invisible to the naked eye.

Captain Willis was well aware that the incursion made by the Dakota would have certainly been enough to put the area on alert. Now, with this contact, they could expect both FRELIMO and ZANLA to turn out in force to search for the Rhodesian's. Should he scrub the mission and call in a couple of helicopters to extract his team before the enemy had chance to close the net? If there were no reported movements of helicopters by either radar or the many eyes and ears scattered throughout the region, FRELIMO would know that the Rhodesian's were still on the ground and maintain their search until they either made contact or assured themselves that the area was clear. It was a dilemma but, Captain Willis weighed up the probable's and decided that the nature of the prize outweighed the risks.

They'd carry on with the operation. His biggest concern now was that the enemy might stop or reroute the convoy.

The plan was to move at least ten miles away from the scene of the contact and re-establish another ambush position in the hope that, even when the mine was triggered, after sweeping the road ahead, ZANLA and their FRELIMO chums would conclude the Rhodesians had been spooked into retreating back across the border. That being the case they'd carry on – while exercising extreme caution – lest more mines had been planted along the way

The SAS were making good progress, but were only a few miles into the move they began to hear the sound of heavy vehicles to their rear. The noise was little more than a low rumble but distinct enough to tell the men that there was a convoy – and a very large convoy at that – approaching. If it was the target ZANLA convoy, then there were far more vehicles than the ones they'd been briefed to expect. Perhaps FRELIMO had joined them along the way? It was also ahead of the predicted schedule which was a cause for concern.

Suddenly the dull thud of an explosion rent the air. The SAS men knew that one of the vehicles had tripped the landmine. What followed shortly after came as a surprise. They could hear ammunition 'cooking off' and this signified that the truck which had hit the mine was carrying ammo. *Although it was unbeknown to the SAS at that time, the vehicles they heard was indeed the ZANLA convoy and, for some incomprehensible reason, whoever was in charge had decided to put a truck loaded with ammo at the head of the convoy.*

Although the enemy was beyond visual range, the SAS could still hear enough to make an accurate appraisal of the situation. In between the intermittent crack and pop of exploding bullets, the noise of trucks reversing and manoeuvring told its own story. Rather than turning and retracing their steps to the nearest FRELIMO base, it appeared the convoy was settling down to wait until the ammo truck and its load had burnt itself out. Finding a piece of high ground which afforded enough of a view over the surrounding bush for their needs, The SAS were at last able to get the convoy in sight. Looking through the binoculars in the dying minutes of that day's sunlight, they caught a glimpse of a few of the trucks. However, when night fell, and headlights were turned on, the SAS men realised that the suspicions they had about the size of the convoy were correct.

There was no way they – a sixteen man strong unit – could hope to attack such a large force. Instead, Captain Willis decided, they would have to turn the task of knocking out the convoy over to the RhAF.

A radio call was put into Rhodesia and the situation was described in detail by way of encrypted Morse. This, Captain Willis emphasised, was a target not to be missed.

Everyone was aware that RhAF resources were

stretched almost beyond capacity and, as such, were only deployed sparingly but the callsign were silently hoping that those in charge would realise the significance of target.

Captain Willis didn't have to wait long for the reply. Both SAS HQ and ComOps (Combined Operations) agreed. The Rhodesian Air Force would arrive at dawn.

The SAS team moved forward into a position where they were better able to direct the airstrikes and ambush any surviving vehicles as they attempted to make their escape.

As first light approached, the ammo truck was still burning and its load still cooking off. It was obvious to the watching SAS and the enemy that it was an impassable obstacle. Realising the danger they were in from Rhodesian planes, ZANLA was preparing to pull out. Engines were started and much noise made as the convoy readied itself for the move back to the safety of the anti-aircraft cover available at the nearest FRELIMO base.

At first the sound of the approaching lone Lynx was lost beneath the revving diesel motors but the terrorists were quick to hear it. Vehicles were called to a stop, lights and engines were extinguished and ZANLA prepared to defend themselves.

Apart from the pilot, the Lynx was carrying Captain Bob McKenzie (he of the Cabora Bassa mission). He was in the front passenger seat and acting as coordinator between the SAS callsign and the RhAF.

On the ground Captain Willis began to speak into the radio handset, guiding the Lynx into position overhead using the burning truck as its reference point.

High overhead, while they saw the flames and smoke from ammo truck, both Captain McKenzie and the pilot were unable to pinpoint the location of the enemy. There were far too many trees and ZANLA were hiding themselves well beneath them. The Pilot decided it was pointless staying at this altitude as they'd never see the terrorists unless they decided to move so, ignoring the obvious danger, he announced he was going to make a low-level pass. Dropping to treetop height, the plane flew directly over the heads of the SAS before passing over the location pointed out to them.

Suddenly, and without warning, the whole area erupted in gunfire. Rifles, machineguns, 12.7mm HMGs, RPG-7s and even the dreaded Soviet made Strela shoulder launched SAM missiles raked the sky.

The Lynx was so low that it was out of sight to the SAS men on the ground and, given the sheer volume of fire, it was apparent that the Lynx could never make it out of the killing zone.

In the Lynx, both the pilot and Captain McKenzie were stunned by the response however, with great presence of mind and razor like reflexes, the pilot threw his plane into a series of violent evasive manoeuvres which saw them escaped the shooting with not so much as a single scratch on the Lynx!

On the ground, the watching SAS men were astounded with the amount of enemy fire they'd just witnessed. It was clear that there were hundreds of ZANLA and FRELIMO on the scene.

As the Lynx was making good its escape a pair of Hunters came screaming in. They had no need to be directed onto the target, they'd seen all the shooting from the trees. Coming under fire themselves, they dropped a clutch of four 1,000lb bombs directly into the centre of the target.

Both aircraft banked hard and climbed. The AA fire had now stopped, the enemy only seemed concerned with escape.

Two more passes saw the Hunters empty their cannons, saturating the target with 30mm cannon fire.

Although they couldn't see properly, the SAS men looked on open mouthed at the scene which had unfolded before them. It was obvious that the RhAF had wreaked havoc among the enemy. Columns of thick black smoke rose from the treetops like oily exclamation marks as the trucks beneath burned. There was the sound of multiple explosions as the loads being carried went up in the flames and, now and then, fireballs erupted skywards as petrol and other combustibles exploded.

As the first pair of Hunters departed another two swept in, bombing, rocketing and strafing the area. Captain Willis and his men could not believe what they were seeing.

The RhAF kept up the attacks until they were sure there was nothing left to shoot at. They came in waves, pair after pair, for several hours, visiting utter devastation upon the enemy.

By the time the planes had gone, the SAS were well on their way out of the area. They knew what form the FRELIMO response would take and didn't want to be around when it happened.

Not long into the move, the SAS realised FRELIMO were tracking them. They'd been quick to get on the callsign's trail and seemed eager to extract revenge for the destruction of the convoy. In this instance, anti-tracking methods were proving no match for the experience of the Freddie. Captain Willis knew there was only one way of bringing the pursuit to a halt, or at least slowing it down enough to allow his team to make good their escape.

The callsign had been changing direction quite randomly for some time as they made their way to their destination. The reason was to confuse any trackers and stop FRELIMO from being able to determine a direction of travel. Now, as they passed through an area where it was impossible not to leave spoor, Captain Willis instructed his men to leave behind a few little surprises. Hidden grenades with instantaneous fuses were carefully placed along the trail. Fine fishing line, virtually invisible to even the keenest eye, was strung across the trail and tied off to the grenade pins which had all but been fully pulled. The slightest touch would result in the grenade exploding and those within its blast radius killed.

Even if they managed to spot the traps, it was odds on that the FRELIMO trackers would slow down. Most of them knew that the Rhodesian's saw them as prize targets and would lay in wait to shoot them dead. This, and the knowledge that many of their ilk had been killed by bullets or bombs already, was enough to have a lot of trackers claim they'd lost the spoor, or take FRELIMO off on a false trail.

As the SAS team pressed on, twice they heard explosions. Someone had tripped the booby traps or had deliberately initiated them to clear the way.

The explosions were quite close – within a mile – giving the callsign a clear indication of the proximity of the pursuing force.

The SAS were making for the DZ into which they'd parachuted. The area was ideal for helicopter landings and, crucially, it meant the team could recover their hidden parachutes (the Rhodesian's would always go to great lengths to bring home their 'chutes as the pressure of sanctions meant they were always in short supply)

Once there they would request an extraction and lay in wait until the RhAF could oblige. The size of the callsign meant that several helicopters were required to airlift them back to Rhodesia.

When they finally arrived at their destination it was becoming clear that FRELIMO was no longer giving chase. That didn't mean the callsign were out of the frying pan though; Freddie could still mount an effective search by simply combing the area in enough strength to get a result.

During a scheduled radio transmission, Captain Willis was informed that his team should return to the site of the convoy to make an assessment of the damage caused. With all the ongoing FRELIMO activity the order wasn't welcomed but, leaving the bulk of his party behind at the DZ under the command of the patrol's 2ic, Captain Willis took four men and picked his way gingerly through the bush. They were expecting to come into contact with FRELIMO every step of the way and, as a result, it took a long time to reach the scene.

Thankfully, there were no FRELIMO to be seen, but the sight which greeted them was one of utter devastation. Burned out trucks, wrecked equipment and body parts lay scattered across the area. The air was thick with smoke from the fires, the grass had been alight and was still smouldering as the SAS men picked their way through the carnage looking for anything of intelligence value.

They came across a consignment of spare parts for Russian made T-34 tanks – the first indication that FRELIMO had deployed armour close to the Rhodesian border.

It was obvious that the dead were FRELIMO, not ZANLA (although a few terrorists were found scattered among the bodies).

Reconnaissance complete, Captain Willis and his team returned to the DZ to be lifted back to Rhodesia the following day.

Through signals intercepts it transpired that, apart from a large convoy carrying brand new equipment (all carried by new trucks) the Rhodesian's had taken out the Headquarters of an entire FRELIMO brigade. The mission had cost FRELIMO and ZANLA dear. They were banking on that equipment, and especially the trucks, to bolster their capabilities but the Rhodesian's had suddenly denied them of it all. It would take many months for the shortfall in materials to be made up, while the loss of the trucks was never made good.

EIGHT: WHO DARES WINS. 1978

1978 was a big year in the history of the Rhodesian SAS. In June of that year C squadron became the 1st Rhodesian Special Air Service Regiment. Expansion of numbers and the addition of new Squadrons meant that the regiment, which was always below strength as C Squadron, needed to recruit more operators to fill its ranks and satisfy the obligations it had in terms of the general war effort.

The usual path into the SAS was through service with other branches of the Rhodesian army; indeed, this was the norm throughout the rest of the SAS family but – with manpower extremely tight – other units (principally the RLI) became intolerant of the SAS 'poaching' their best and most experienced men.

To get around this the SAS came up with an innovative yet controversial plan; it would allow candidates who had no previous military experience to undertake its selection process. The pool of potential recruits was to be drawn from the ranks of the National Service personnel who had been drafted into the army for their compulsory military service. These young men, only eighteen years of age, could volunteer to try their hand at selection at the beginning of their basic training.

The plan was that, rather than rely on skills taught by other units, the SAS would be able to train these candidates to their own exacting standards during a gruelling six-month course.

From the outset the programme was designed to be even tougher than the already arduous SAS selection course which experienced troops had to attend. As a result the failure rates were very high, especially so in the early stages, when those deemed unfit for SAS service for whatever reason were ruthlessly weeded out.

With a success rate hovering around the 5% mark, only the best of the best of the best candidates made it through to the end to be passed on for active service with one of the Squadrons. Passing selection did not mean becoming an SAS operator though. The new recruits had one final obstacle to overcome before they were allowed to wear the sand beret, winged dagger badge and SAS stable belt; they had to prove their worth to their Squadron mates on live operations.

One unforeseen bonus of this programme was that the SAS were sending all its failed candidates on to serve with other units and, especially if they'd managed to stay on the course beyond the initial basic training phase, those units were receiving young men who were highly trained and motivated.

In practice, the NS recruit programme proved a success but later on, when the war situation deteriorated and the need to get SAS troops became even more pressing, the six-month training and selection course was pared down to just four. Four months to turn out someone who was capable of operating to SAS standards was first seen as an impossibility, but it is a testament to the training staff that they managed to do it with no loss of quality among the young men they were sending on to serve with the regiment.

Throughout 1978 the SAS was heavily engaged in Mozambique, fighting a successful campaign against ZANLA and FRELIMO. However, other areas of concern were emerging which required SAS attention.

In Zambia, although active, ZIPRA had been quietly biding their time, building up their forces while allowing the rival ZANLA to bear the brunt of Rhodesian attacks.

They'd also been pushing men across the border into Botswana (on Rhodesia's least defended western border) where they were mounting small-scale incursions.

Now, as the bush war heated up to boiling point, it was time for the SAS to act and put paid to Joshua Nkomo's plans for the communist takeover of Rhodesia.

The ZIPRA who had arrived in Botswana were declaring themselves as refugees and until the SAS made to cut off their main method of infiltration (by sinking the ferry between Zambia and Botswana) operations on Botswanan soil were largely restricted to intelligence gathering.

In Zambia, where overt support for ZIPRA from the authorities was the order of the day, the situation was different. In response to the increasing threat from the Soviet backed terrorists, the Rhodesian security forces began to step up their efforts to defeat ZIPRA.

Meanwhile, most people (rightly at the time) considered the main terrorist menace to lay with ZANLA operating out of Mozambique. While, ZIPRA enjoyed the patronage of the Zambian's, the Zambian military never actively supported them in their fight against Rhodesia. As has been described already, in Mozambique it was different.

Siphoning off troops and other assets from the 'eastern front' to fight ZIPRA meant that the under resourced RSF came under even more strain in their campaign against ZANLA. By 1978, ZANLA (and sometimes FRELIMO) were making numerous incursions across the border and deep into the Rhodesian heartlands, carrying out ever more numerous attacks on the civilian population as well as the county's communications network and infrastructure. Instead of trying to chase and stop the terrorist gangs once they were inside Rhodesia, it had long been the case that, wherever possible, it was best that the threat should be neutralised at source.

The attacks on enemy camps and supply chains was proved to have a detrimental effect on the terrorist's ability to mount offensive operations but now, as the war escalated even further, it became a priority. Concentrating RSF assets in these types of attacks was an economical and effective use of the scant resources available to the

Rhodesian's.

The RSF took a lot of prisoners, The vast majority fell into their hands in the usual manner, while others (high ranking ZAPU/ZANU and ZIPRA/ZANLA officials) who, by virtue of their access to secrets, the Rhodesian's knew would make valuable prizes for the CIO and Special Branch, were earmarked for kidnap. These 'snatch' missions were often carried out by the Selous Scouts but sometimes undertaken by CIO agents or the SAS. Such operations soon proved to be a vital component in the ongoing intelligence war.

One such target of the snatch teams was a high ranking ZANLA official. A Selous Scouts team operating in the Tete province of Mozambique had snatched the man from his bed and spirited him across the border into Rhodesia where he was delivered to the CIO.

Once in captivity the man proved to be most cooperative. He was quick to denounce his comrades and share the wealth of secret information he'd been privy to.

Whilst collating the information the captive had divulged, CIO officers had their interest piqued by one particular item. The ZANLA official had spoken about a hitherto unknown camp which ZANLA were using as a staging post to push large groups of men across the border into north-eastern Rhodesia. It would be prudent, the CIO thought, if this particular camp could become the focus of RSF attention because its destruction and the deaths of all those in it, would disrupt ZANLA operations in a sector of the front which the Rhodesian's were finding it increasingly difficult to provide a response.

What marked this camp out was the fact that the captive had told the CIO that it was not only important for feeding terrorists into Rhodesia, but also the home to the regional headquarters of ZANU. That being the case there'd be several high ranking officials ripe for capture or elimination, another principal consideration being the top-secret ZANU files which were sure to be stored there for the HQs use; taking them as well as scalps would inevitably prove a coup for the intelligence people.

When details of the camp were passed to the SAS it quickly became clear that it wouldn't be as easy a task as some may have first imagined. The main cause of concern was the geography of the place. It was situated close to the regional capital, Tete, which was home to at least one thousand FRELIMO. The SAS knew full well that the aggressive Freddie would not allow the Rhodesian's to mount an attack so near to the town. Once they realised what was happening their response would be swift and merciless.

Poring over the RhAF reconnaissance photographs and the features which the interpreters had pointed out, plus detailed accounts from the CIO captive, there was even more cause for concern. The target camp was situated on the banks of the Zambezi and right next door was a small FRELIMO outpost and just a short distance away was a barracks housing a Company sized detachment of FRELIMO. When questioned, the ZANLA captive confirmed that these two places were in constant use by Freddie. So, as well as the occupants of the target camp (who, the captive assured them, always numbered approximately 100 men – excluding the ZANU HQ staff), the SAS raiding party would have perhaps the same number again of FRELIMO intervening immediately the attack commenced and potentially another 1,000 or more turning up as soon as they could be mobilised.

The SAS would only have a small number of men available for the task and would have to rely on stealth and surprise to carry it off.

It would take a great deal of lateral thinking to successfully take out the target camp and those in it then escape before FRELIMO could become embroiled.

I have already spoken about the difficulties the Rhodesian's faced when operating in the Tete province. The FRELIMO air defences and heavy presence of ground forces throughout the forward areas of the province meant that an airborne assault would be seen on radar screens or FRELIMO on the ground before it could get anywhere near the target. Even if RhAF aircraft managed to run the gauntlet of AA fire without loss, the whole area would be alerted and, by the time they reached the target, ZANLA would have probably vacated it.

It was the target's location on the Zambezi which gave the SAS planners their break. Instead of sending a fleet of helicopters directly against the camp, they could be used instead to deposit the SAS far enough away from it so as not to cause any concern. Given the concentrations of AA assets it would still be a dangerous move, but far less risky than the alternative. So, once deposited, how would the SAS make the long approach to the target?

Selecting a HLZ close to the Zambezi and upstream of the target would allow the SAS to make their approach along the great river in Klepper canoes.

Once at the target, the plan was to destroy it and everyone in it, before they knew what was happening. To this end, plans to take ZANU prisoners or documents from the HQ were abandoned; the SAS would make sure they all went up in smoke instead.

After approaching under cover of darkness from upriver, in the early hours of the morning the SAS raiding force would land on the perimeter of the camp which bordered the Zambezi. They knew from the recce photos that there were no physical obstacles between the river and the camp; the terrorists felt no need to defend from that quarter, after all the river formed the perfect natural barrier and no one could ever attack from that direction?

By the time the raiding party arrived, the camps occupants (and the neighbouring FRELIMO) would all be tucked up in bed asleep. The SAS had the CIO question their captive about guard routines and were informed that

ZANLA always had three men on night duty but they never patrolled the facility, instead they stayed at the front gate.

So, after leaving the Klepper's, the SAS would creep into the camp and lay chain-linked explosives along the walls of each accommodation block, the ZAPU HQ, a couple of buildings which were used as stores, the armoury, a few ancillary buildings plus – if they had time – the few vehicles which were laagered up. They would then return to the boats and disappear down river without anyone knowing they had been.

The explosives themselves would be fitted with timing devices which would ensure they all exploded at the same time and time was what the SAS needed to make good their escape. A little way down river was the neighbouring FRELIMO barracks. Like the target camp, it too abutted the Zambezi meaning that, if they were seen, the raiding party could be engaged. In the Klepper's it would be difficult to avoid incoming fire and impossible to shoot back so stealth was only real defence. If they got past the barracks there was one last obstacle; a road bridge spanning the Zambezi. The SAS knew that it was guarded at all times by a FRELIMO detachment but were assured by the CIO that Freddie maintained that guard to stop attacks from either end and not from the river. So, with luck, there'd be no one on the bridge looking out across the water to spot the SAS team as they paddled their way towards it.

Once clear of that last hurdle it would be plain sailing all the way to safety.

Appreciations were made as to the length of the delayed action detonators to give the SAS team plenty of time to clear the area before the explosive charges went off. The explosives themselves which were to be used against the buildings were Rhodesian made 'wrecker' charges; these immensely powerful devices were specially designed to demolish structures. Having them placed against the walls of the targets would mean that when they exploded, the collapse of the buildings was assured, those inside would have no chance of escape before they were killed by flying debris or buried under the rubble.

It was a very good plan. The SAS should be in and out without firing a single shot. The first thing FRELIMO would know about it is when they were suddenly woken up by the ear-splitting boom of plastic explosive tearing open the peace of the night.

Captain Dave Dodson (nom de guerre) had come up with the concept of using the Zambezi as a highway with which to attack the ZANLA camp when the operation had first been given to the SAS. He recalled the way the men operating on the Cabora Bassa had been able to operate with virtual impunity because the enemy did not know and never even thought that the Rhodesian's were using the lake to move around the region. As a result he was assigned as commander.

Captain Dobson was a highly respected SAS officer who participated in many of C Squadron's and later 1st SAS' most notable missions. He was known to the SAS by his real name but, given that he chose to use an alias for reasons (the author presumes) surrounding the personal security of his family members means that – even after the passage of time – he will be referred to by the nom de guerre here and his highly impressive SAS service details not gone into detail.

With his plan given approval, Captain Dobson set to work refining it. While in essence the plan was simple, it was fraught with danger. For FRELIMO not to have any notion of what was happening, the infiltration phase would mean a long journey along the Zambezi, with all the possibilities for compromise from patrolling FRELIMO and civilians that entailed.

Captain Dobson decided that an eight-man team, operating from four Klepper's was both large enough to carry out the mission yet small enough to evade the attention of FRELIMO on the infiltration and exfiltration.

He set to work recruiting seven men and together they set off to Lake McIlwaine to brush up on their canoe handling skills on the lake and rivers feeding into it.

Much time was also devoted to practicing placing and arming the wreckers. It had been decided that each charge would be fitted with multiple fuses to (hopefully) eliminate the possibility of them failing to go off. After much deliberation it was also decided that the timers would be set for ninety-minutes, this was a trade-off between allowing the SAS time to escape and lessening the chance of someone discovering the explosives.

When all the rehearsals and preparations were complete, Captain Dobson and his men were moved to an FOB close to the Rhodesia/Mozambique border from where they would deploy by helicopter to the start point close to the Zambezi.

Given the amount of kit and over 550lbs of plastic explosives the team were taking in, they could not be moved by one chopper. The only aircraft available was the small capacity Alouette. This meant that three were required to make the lift (two to carry the SAS men and the third for their equipment). The noise footprint of the Alouette was particularly large and distinctive; to have a trio of them flying low then depositing troops into an area which was populated by a smattering of kraals was sure to result in them being heard, if not seen. The SAS knew only too well that the locals would report the incident to FRELIMO as quickly as they were able and that would result in Freddie being placed on the alert and turning out in force to investigate.

To offset this problem, another SAS callsign was to accompany Captain Dobson's team in a forth Alouette. Landed away from the main HLZ, their job was to provide a distraction by using a medium mortar they took along to 'stonk' a nearby ZANLA staging post. It was hoped that subjecting the place to a brief but heavy barrage of HE bombs might just convince Freddie that the helicopters had come in to drop off the mortar crew and nothing more, a bonus being they might kill or incapacitate a few ZANLA into the bargain. To escape the inevitable FRELIMO reaction, the mortar team would be airlifted out of the area at dawn the next day after they had completed their mission.

Even if the diversion worked, everyone in the area would be alert to the fact that Rhodesian troops may still be in the vicinity, so extreme caution would have to be exercised by the raiding party as they paddled downriver to the objective.

Given the nature of the topography the helicopters would be passing over, and the fact that it was a no moon period, night flying was out of the question. Irrespective of that, it was vital that the raiding party get on to the river and clear the area and they could only do that under cover of darkness. Therefore, the decision was made to carry out the insertion during late afternoon. This would not only give the SAS a good head start, but allow the choppers to return to base while there was still light enough to see by.

Final equipment checks were made. Everything was treble checked then checked once more; if anything was missing of not working properly, the time to discover it was now, not when the SAS were behind enemy lines.

The Alouettes took off and flew together, keeping as low as possible over the densely forested ground. If FRELIMO radar hadn't already spotted them, it was a safe bet that ZANLA or FRELIMO on the ground would have and be rushing to radio in the sighting to their superiors.

Shortly before the main party were due to land, the Alouette carrying the mortar team peeled off to deposit its payload.

The remaining helicopters came in to the HLZ and

waited while the SAS men disembarked and removed their equipment. The choppers were then airborne, climbing and turning for home.

As the noise receded Captain Dobson and his men were convinced that there was no way they had made it this far without being seen. The priority now was to clear the immediate area, but do so tactically. Weighed down by the explosives, and the Klepper's, plus their personal equipment, the SAS men struck out for the mighty Zambezi.

They reached the riverbank in good time and without incident. The Zambezi was in full flow and this fact would make the trip more hazardous than ever.

With one man on lookout, the others set to work assembling the canoes. Apart from the two-man crew, each Klepper was loaded with almost 130lbs of explosives, personal equipment and weapons. Just for good measure each boat had an RPD light machinegun aboard plus a few spare 100-round ammo drums. As a result the Klepper's would be sitting very low in the water and sluggish to respond.

The SAS team waited until well after last light before launching the boats. Instead of paddling into the centre of the river, where the current was strongest, they stayed close to the bank. This way it would be easier to control the canoes as well as make it more difficult to be seen. They were all disguised as ZANLA, wearing the typical terrorist garb and Black is Beautiful skin paint, but it was unlikely that, if spotted, they would get away without being reported. The start point for the journey was approximately fifty miles from the target, there was to be no rushing, the journey would be completed in stages.

Some time into the journey they encountered an area of white water. Given the fact that the boats were so heavily laden they team had no choice but to connect the

Klepper's side by side to form a 'raft' of sorts. They also had to break from cover and go further out to where the river was flowing hardest. Fortunately, the raft trick worked and the little flotilla made it safely though to the far end of the rapids.

Perhaps inevitably, the next obstacle faced by the raiding party was a herd of hippopotamus that were milling about in the shallows. The SAS heard the hippos long before they spotted them through the NV scope. Unlike previous encounters between these huge beasts and waterborne SAS, the Zambezi was wide enough to allow the raiding party to paddle well clear and continue their journey without inciting the wrath of the hippos.

As the first flicker of daylight began to creep across the horizon, the SAS pulled into the bank and, after pulling the Klepper's clear of the water and into good cover, settled down into their LUP routines.

A coded message was sent to SAS HQ which provided a detailed situation report. It was so far so good. The team had not encountered any locals, FRELIMO or ZANLA. They had made good progress along the river and were now more than halfway to the target. One good push during the next leg would see them at the objective with plenty time to carry out the operation. They were informed in turn that the diversionary mortar attack had taken place and intercepted FRELIMO radio traffic confirmed that the hunt for the Rhodesian's was being concentrated in that area. As far as the signals intelligence people could gather, there was no inkling of the raiding party's presence among FRELIMO.

The rest of the day passed uneventfully and, after dark, the SAS took to the Klepper's for the next leg.

In order to speed up the voyage, Captain Dobson decided to go mid-river, using the fast flowing current to the raiding party's advantage. Here, they would hardly have to paddle at all, the force of the river speeding them along all the way.

As predicted, the rapidity with which the river was flowing meant that the team began to close on the target camp with plenty of time to spare to carry out the attack and make good their escape. Every man knew what he was doing and what his responsibilities were so there was no need to stop and make final preparations, it was green for go all the way in.

The river forced itself into a rather sharp bend a few hundred yards before the ZANLA camp. As they approached from beyond the curve, the SAS team could see some lights. This, they knew, was the FRELIMO outpost and the neighbouring target.

As the team rounded the bend they were confronted with a sight none of them were expecting. The FRELIMO outpost was well illuminated in the darkness – far too well illuminated for security purposes – but some of the lights were shining out across the river. They were powerful lamps which cast solid light right across the width of the Zambezi and onto the far bank.

The SAS were suddenly in a quandary; even if they moved to the far side of the river, they'd still be well within the glare of the lights. It would only take a FRELIMO sentry to glance out across the water to spot them and raise the alarm. There was no way of back-paddling out of sight to a spot where they could appraise the situation because the current was simply too strong. As they floated inexorably towards the light, Captain Dobson made a snap decision; the team would stay in mid-channel and allow the fast flowing water to carry them through.

Getting as low as possible in the Klepper's so as to reduce their profiles, the SAS men watched and waited as their boats drifted into the lamplight. All eyes were on the FRELIMO outpost. They were looking for movement or anything else which would tell them they'd been seen. Every man was expecting to hear a shout followed by gunshots. They had their own weapons at the ready and were waiting to reply with a fusillade of their own.

If things suddenly went noisy the team knew it would only signify the start of their troubles. Once alerted, there was no way they could hope to make it past the FRELIMO barracks and the bridge. The only hope would be to beach the Klepper's just after they'd passed the target camp and then go into full evasion mode. With the FRELIMO from Tete town joining in the hunt, it would be very difficult to stay one step ahead of the enemy and get into a position where they could safely call in a helicopter to extract them.

Miraculously the SAS team made it beyond the overspill of light without being seen. FRELIMO must have been so sure that no threat could ever materialise by way of the river that they didn't even bother to look (either that or the guards were asleep – which was also a distinct possibility).

Back in the embrace of the darkness, the raiding party took to the paddles making gentle strokes to nose the Klepper's towards the bank. They beached the canoes, alighted then began to prepare their demolition charges. Here, among some scrub on the bank side about halfway between the FRELIMO outpost and the ZANLA camp they were safe from view. Like its neighbour, the ZANLA camp was lit up, although the lights had been erected so as to illuminate the camp itself rather than the approaches to it. ZANLA really knew how to make this facility into one which could be easily shot up in the dark! The gift of light meant the SAS men were able to do a detailed visual appraisal of the place. There was no activity, and certainly no patrolling sentries. Leaving a couple of men behind to guard the boats, the rest of the raiding party moved forward along the shoreline, alternating between keeping eyes on the target and the river bank in case of crocodiles.

As expected, there was no fence running along the water's edge and the SAS were able to enter the camp simply by easing themselves around the place where the perimeter fence ended.

They moved forward and began the process of laying the wreckers against the walls of each of the buildings, doing so to a chorus of snores emanating from within.

As they were planting the charges on one of the barrack's sides they were given a start when a naked ZANLA terrorist appeared through the door. The SAS men froze and looked on as he urinated then disappeared back inside.

With the explosives laid and the delayed action fuses initiated, the raiders withdrew silently to where the Klepper's were hidden. They now had less than seventy minutes to make good their escape.

No sooner than the SAS team had gotten mid-river for their exfiltration, the night was shattered by a thunderclap of explosions. For some unknown reason the wreckers had detonated far too early. Looking back, the raiders saw flames and a huge finger of smoke curling up towards the night sky. Such was the sudden intensity of the fires that they illuminated the river all the way down to the bridge.

At the FRELIMO barracks, the alarm went up. Someone was beating what sounded like a sheet of metal suspended on rope, makeshift gong fashion. As the SAS looked on they could see bemused Freddie's turning out all over the camp. From where they were on the river, and given the flickering orange light being cast across the scene, any one of the barracks inhabitants would be able to spot them should they look in their direction.

Thankfully, not one man looked to see if anything was happening on the water.

With the barracks now behind them, the final and most dangerous obstacle was yet to be overcome.

The road bridge loomed large ahead. Keen to make as little movement as possible, the SAS men stopped paddling, allowing the current to carry them down river.

Up on the bridge they could see movement; men were running across the span in both directions, seemingly in a panic. They were all armed with rifles and one glance down at the water would mean the raiders would quickly come under heavy fire. The SAS team held their breaths as they trained their own weapons on the enemy; they all had authority to initiate a contact if they knew they'd been seen. All hell would have let lose at that point, with the SAS raking the bridge with rifle and RPD fire and FRELIMO shooting back.

Soon the Klepper's floated out of sight beneath the bridge; beyond, a shadow was being cast by the structure in the raging light of the fires. With luck, everyone up on top would keep doing what they were already doing, pointing, shouting and staring out at the ZANLA camp as they tried to figure out among themselves what had happened and what their reaction should be.

As quickly as the bridge appeared it was behind them. Carried along in the central current, the hullabaloo quickly faded out of earshot.

When they knew they were safe from being seen or heard, the SAS men began to paddle. With the explosives gone, the Klepper's were a delight to handle and onwards the little flotilla quickly pushed towards their next objective.

The final destination was about twelve miles away from the bridge and the SAS team made good time before paddling to the shore. While two men stood guard the others began the task of breaking down the Klepper's ready for the final phase of the operation. A radio signal was sent back to SAS HQ telling that the job had been successfully completed.

The raiders retreated into cover to await the helicopters which they knew were waiting on standby to extract them.

A couple of hours after daybreak two Alouettes came

scudding in low over the bush. Guided in by their Becker homing devices which, in turn, were responding to the callsign's radio man's transmission. A HLZ had been surveyed and cleared of obstacles and, once visual contact was established, the SAS guided the choppers in onto their location. No time was wasted as it was clear that FRELIMO would have been tracking the aircraft on their radar screens. Given what had happened only a few hours earlier, the whole area would be on alert and the area thick with enemy.

With the Klepper's, the men and their kit aboard, the Alouettes made rolling takeoffs, lifting into the early morning sky. As they began the journey home, both choppers suddenly found themselves under fire from what they suspected to be a FRELIMO patrol. Freddie was too far away to have any impact but it was a reminder to all that the enemy was out there searching.

After arriving back at the FOB, the callsign were debriefed and instructed to compile their after action reports.

Intercepted FRELIMO and ZANLA radio traffic revealed that, unfortunately for the SAS, the terrorist camp was not full when they struck. Instead of the 100 plus casualties they were hoping for, there were less than thirty present (including a few from ZANU). A high altitude RhAF reconnaissance overfly revealed that the camp itself had been more or less completely destroyed by the SAS. All the barracks blocks were collapsed, as was the ZANU HQ building. The photographs taken revealed that the fires and secondary explosions had (predictably) originated from the armoury and stores.

The premature detonation of the explosives was never satisfactorily explained. All the timers had been rigorously tested prior to their use. The only thing the SAS could do was record the failure of the timers and hope the problem – whatever it was – could be resolved before their next use.

Other radio transmissions which were deciphered by the Rhodesian signals intelligence people revealed that neither FRELIMO nor ZANLA had the slightest inkling of how the Rhodesian's had managed to attack the camp. They never made the connection between the Zambezi and the mission.

Despite the disappointment that they were unable to eliminate more terrorists, the SAS knew that the operation had been a stunning success. The very fact that they has managed to strike at a target almost in the suburbs of the regional capital of Tete province had shaken both FRELIMO and ZANLA. Up to that point they were convinced that the town and the military facilities surrounding it were immune to Rhodesian attack, simply by virtue of their location and the strength of defences. They were suddenly forced to confront the reality that the Rhodesian's were able to strike wherever they liked whenever they liked.

Of course, the thing which really stymied FRELIMO was their complete inability to understand the nature of Special Forces operations. Their military doctrines were rooted firmly in the communist mould and their way of thinking followed the same path. To them, for anyone to attack a target such as the ZANLA camp would require a large force of men moving in overland – and certainly not just eight highly trained operators sneaking in behind everyone's backs in canoes.

NINE: DAY OF DAYS. 1978

The realisation that ZIPRA was stepping up its campaign of terror was brought into sharp focus when one of its gangs used a Russian supplied Strela shoulder launched surface to air missile to shoot down a Rhodesian Airways Viscount passenger plane. The aircraft was on a scheduled flight and only carrying civilians. As the stricken aircraft burned and plunged to earth, the pilot attempted a forced landing but the nature of the ground was such that it proved impossible. Incredibly, there were eighteen survivors, including some children and two air hostesses. Injured and dazed, they stumbled out of the blazing wreckage and into the bush. Before long the ZIPRA Strela gang appeared on the scene and began to shoot the survivors. Two of those who had escaped the burning plane (including an incredibly brave air hostess by the name of Dianne Hansen) managed to evade the terrorists.

The two survivors spent the night in the bush. The following morning, when the missing plane was found, an SAS callsign parachuted into the location to access the situation on the ground. The pair were found and brought to safety.

It wasn't the first time the terrorists had attempted to shoot down a civilian aircraft with the batch of Strela missiles the Soviets had supplied, but the first which had been successful for them.

Operating from inside Zambia, a ZIPRA Strela gang launched a missile against a twin engined Piper Aztec light aircraft which was carrying five tourists on a sightseeing flight over Victoria Falls. Fortunately for those aboard, even though the Strela was the latest '2M' version, it was still rather inaccurate and easily fooled if other heat sources were present.

The ZIPRA gang tracked the Piper as it flew sedately

over the area around the falls before the leader gave the order to fire.

Once launched, the missile was diverted away from the aircraft as it flew low over the Elephant Hills Hotel by the heat issuing from the building's air conditioning system. The result being that the hotel was struck and the kitchens set ablaze. The fire quickly spread and destroyed a large portion of the hotel.

It was when they later learned what had happened with the errant missile that ZIPRA realised they needed to target larger commercial aircraft.

The incident had shocked and enraged the Rhodesian population, especially when it was revealed that the survivors had been executed. The outrage peaked when Nkomo acknowledged that ZIPRA was responsible (though he denied the shooting of the surviving passengers – including the children)

In response to the reaction of the people of Rhodesia the government was quick to announce that it would hunt down an eliminate those responsible.

As far as the military planners were concerned this meant everyone in the ZIPRA machine; from Joshua Nkomo to the newest terrorist recruit.

Although the SAS had been hard at work inside Zambia, their operations were largely confined to small unit actions; for example targeting ZIPRA by way of ambush or minelaying on their forward lines of communication. There had been some attacks on terrorist camps but that was still quite a rare occurrence.

Now the new 1st (Rhodesian) Special Air Service Regiment was determined to take part in ComOps plans to punish ZIPRA and shatter its ability to mount offensive operations.

Instead of making piecemeal attacks which did little but nibble away at the edges of the Soviet backed terror machine, the Rhodesian planners decided that it would be best to target ZIPRA en masse; principally at their training and holding camps. These camps were often large, some holding many thousands of terrorists in various stages of training or who were waiting to be deployed over the border into Rhodesia.

The main problem was that the bulk of the ZIPRA camps were sited deep inside Zambia, which created inevitable logistical problems for the over-stretched Rhodesian security forces. The Leader of ZIPRA, Joshua Nkomo, was well aware of Rhodesian limitations and craftily made a point of positioning said camps where he knew them to be beyond the reach of RSF ground troops.

The main ZIPRA Camp in Zambia was called FC (Freedom Camp – AKA Westlands Farm) which was sited – purposely – about ten miles north of the Zambian capital, Lusaka. FC was a sprawling facility, home to no less than 4,000 ZIPRA terrorists. FC was also the main base for the ZIPRA high command. Rhodesian intelligence knew that this was where all ZIPRA operations against Rhodesia were planned.

Nkomo had chosen the location of FC well; any Rhodesian aircraft wishing to attack the site would have to run the gauntlet of Zambian AA defences which were positioned to protect Lusaka. Apart from the usual AA guns, the Zambian military were equipped with British supplied Rapier SAM missiles. The Rapier was a modern and very sophisticated weapons system which posed a considerable threat to any RhAF aircraft that penetrated Zambian airspace. Combined with a powerful search and tracking radar network and bolstered by other, older, missiles meant that Nkomo was confident that FC would not come under air attack.

There were two other important ZIPRA camps which, up to this point in time, had been considered 'out of bounds' by the Rhodesian military by virtue of their location. One was known as Mkushi and the other CGT-2 (Communist Guerrilla Training Camp number two).

Mkushi was even further into the Zambian heartland than FC, being situated some ninety-five miles north-east of Lusaka. Given its location, not much was known about Mkushi, save for the fact that ZIPRA regarded it as a principal asset. RhAF reconnaissance photos revealed there were at least 1,000 ZIPRA present at the camp.

CGT-2 was another vast complex, about sixty miles east of Lusaka. As the name suggests, its purpose was to train terrorists for deployment into Rhodesia (training which was overseen by Russian and East German 'advisors').

All three sites had enjoyed an existence free from the prospect of molestation from the Rhodesian security forces but, as ComOps looked to dismantle the ZIPRA threat and punish them for what they'd done to the airliner, that was all set to change.

The ComOps planners decided they should hit ZIPRA hard with a series of carefully co-ordinated attacks from both air and ground forces and the SAS was to form a vital component of the operation.

While Nkomo and the wider ZIPRA hierarchy were relying on geography and Zambian air defences to keep them safe the Rhodesian's knew differently. Although it would require maximum effort from the RhAF and soak up almost all the rotary wing capability, with careful planning, it was just possible to mount almost simultaneous attacks by ground troops on both Mkushi and CGT-2. As for FC, that would be attended to by RhAF Canberra bombers and Hunters.

Experience told the Rhodesian's that the Zambian's were most reluctant to use their SAM missiles against RhAF targets for fear of the reprisals it would bring. They did, on occasion, shoot at aircraft with their traditional AA guns but those incidents were few and far between.

That said, the RhAF could not afford to be complacent; it was vital that they steered clear of Lusaka because they knew that would provoke a response which would probably include the launching of Rapiers or the Soviet built SAMs. Just as long as the Zambian's were aware that the targets were ZIPRA and not themselves, the RhAF were confident they should get away without being targeted.

There was, of course, the small question of the Zambian Air Force (ZAF). It was small but quite well equipped. Mostly operating obsolete aircraft, it did field some Mig-17 and 19 fighters but they were always nowhere to be seen, especially when the sidewinder equipped RhAF Hunters were about.

ZIPRA had its own air defence capabilities which were bolstered over time by the Russians. Apart from towed 23mm guns, the Strela shoulder launched SAM was appearing in ever greater numbers. Obviously, unlike the Zambian's, ZIPRA had no qualms about opening fire on the RhAF. It was a given that the three target camps would be defended by some 23mm guns, HMGs and small arms but quite likely that Strela's would also be encountered, so the Rhodesian's expected come under fire from the ground as they made their attacks.

Freedom Camp would be the first to be hit. With all the strength they could muster, the RhAF would bomb the camp, dropping 500lb HE, Alpha bouncing bombs and Frantan (Frangible Tank) bombs each containing 100 gallons of napalm. The idea was to flatten the place and kill or incapacitate as many of the occupants as possible before they could disperse and set what was left ablaze.

That the Rhodesian's were in possession of a detailed layout of the camp meant they could strike where they knew it would cause most havoc. One of the priorities was the ZIPRA high command. Taking out the buildings which housed them and their offices would be done at the very start of the airstrike then, when the bewildered

ZIPRA footsoldiers were scrambling out of their beds, RhAF Canberra bombers would streak low overhead to deposit the deadly Alpha bombs across the camp. Each Canberra could carry no less than 300 Alpha bombs in its bomb bay and, spread out among the fleeing terrorists, they would cause carnage. The Hunters would finish off by dropping the Frantan's across the camp and raking any surviving ZIPRA with 30mm cannon fire. Within minutes, the destruction of FC would be more or less complete.

The aircraft would then return to Rhodesia to be rearmed and refuelled before taking off for Mkushi.

Immediately after the same treatment was meted out to Mkushi and its eight satellite camps, a force totalling 165 SAS troops (virtually the whole of the Regiment) were to be deployed by static-line parachute and helicopter.

The plan was to conduct a Fireforce style attack, surrounding the main camp before moving in to destroy it and its inhabitants. Now, we have to understand that the physical size of Mkushi camp and the small numbers of SAS available meant that the act of encircling to the point where no one could escape was impossible. The SAS would have to do the best they could and hope to catch those escaping with stop groups.

There was also the small matter of the 1,000 ZIPRA. Some would certainly have been killed in the initial airstrike, while others were able to make good their escape as the SAS were deploying, but – and even if the intelligence estimates were correct – that could leave the SAS outnumbered at least three, perhaps four or even five to one. Experience told the Rhodesian's that the terrorists would all be well armed and that the camp itself defended by machinegun positions and, perhaps, trenches. Standard military tactics dictate that an attacking force should outnumber the defenders by at least two to one but, for the SAS, the fact that they were severely outnumbered was path of the course.

The distances involved between Mkushi and Rhodesia meant that the Alouettes could not fly to the target and back, therefore a secret staging post was to be established some way south of the target camp which would allow them to refuel and, in the case of the 'K' cars ('Kill' cars; Alouettes which had been converted into the gunship role by the fitting of a sideways firing 20mm cannon) be rearmed.

As far as CGT-2 was concerned, an attack timed to occur a couple of hours after the one on Mkushi had gotten underway. A force of RLI was going to be para-dropped immediately after an RhAF airstrike. Given the constraints placed upon it by the two other camp attacks, the only aircraft available to hit CGT-2 were a few elderly Vampire jet fighter-bombers, some Lynx's and Alouette K cars. The Vampire could only carry a single 500lb bomb or light rockets. While it also had four 20mm cannon, by virtue of its limited bomb load it was unsuited to the task of effectively attacking the sprawling ZIPRA camp, as indeed was the lightly armed Lynx. Still, they were the only force the RhAF could muster for the task, so would have to suffice. Just like the SAS attacking Mkushi, there was only a small force of RLI commandos available for the job of dealing with ZIPRA on the ground; for the RLI, facing up to 4,000 terrorists, the odds stacked against them would be even worse.

The scale of the operation to attack the three main ZIPRA camps had soaked up meagre Rhodesian resources but, if the men involved managed to pull it off, they would deal a blow to Nkomo's terror machine from which it would never fully recover.

Everything had to be kept secret as men were assembled and aircraft prepared.

As the final preparations were being made, a piece of

intelligence arrived at ComOps. The CIO had learned that none other than Joshua Nkomo himself and some members of his high command were due to attend a passing out parade of ZIPRA recruits at Freedom Camp.

This was an opportunity not to be missed, as well as killing a sizable number of terrorists, the Rhodesian's had a chance to eliminate the 'fat man' himself.

The operation was postponed for three days so that it coincided with the arrival of Nkomo and the passing out parade.

The SAS had been preparing furiously for their attack on Mkushi. Every available man was drafted in to take part, including TF troops. In total there were 270 SAS taking part, not all directly involved in the attack, but carrying out various vitally important support roles. As a result, the task of manning the staging post, from where the helicopters involved in the Mkushi operation could be refuelled was mostly given over to the RLI. In turn, so short of men were the commandos that they had only newly qualified recruits for the job. These men had only just completed their static-line parachute course and the drop into the 'admin base' would be their first operational jump.

The day that 'Operation Gatling' was to be launched finally arrived. It was only a few days previously, safely quarantined in their various barracks and FOBs, which those involved were made aware of what they were about to do. The mission objectives were read out to those involved in the ground operations against Mkushi and CGT-2; the killing of as many terrorists as possible, the capture of any high-ranking or otherwise important ZIPRA/ZAPU officials, the destruction of the camps (especially the communications centres and supply facilities), the gathering of intelligence by way of documentation and other sources and the destruction of all recovered terrorist weaponry and ordnance.

The operation began with the air attack on Freedom Camp. Canberras and Hunters made their way low and fast into the interior of Zambia, skirting Lusaka's air defences all the way. With a pair of Hunters providing high cover against possible intervention by the ZAF MiGs, the Hunters went in first, dropping the Frantan napalm canisters and HE bombs. They were closely followed by the Canberras delivering thousands of Alpha bombs across the area. The terrorists attending the passing out parade had no idea what was happening and, caught in the middle of the storm of fire and explosions, panicked then scattered, running for cover in every direction. Their bomb bays empty, the Canberras turned for home but not before the leader of the attack, Squadron Leader Chris Dixon, had his now legendary exchange with Zambian air traffic controllers (*For your information, at the time of writing the audio recording of the attack on FC and the subsequent conversation between Squadron Leader Dixon and the Zambian air traffic controllers is available to listen to on YouTube – simply search 'Greenleader raid'. Note: it's best listened to through headphones.*) The Hunters made several more passes, strafing the fleeing terrorists with 30mm cannon fire while predatory K-cars swept the perimeters shooting at targets of opportunity.

The devastation was total and, when the RhAF left the scene, Freedom Camp was in ruins. Fortunately, ZIPRA had no time with which to mount a defence against the Rhodesian aircraft; no Strela's were fired and the AA guns which had shown up on RhAF reconnaissance photos, proved to be dummies.

The priority now was a return to Rhodesia and a rapid turnaround so the second airstrike of the day could be mounted against Mkushi.

The SAS were waiting for the off. The helicopter borne troops would take off first while those to be para-dropped into the target were to leave later. It was all carefully co-ordinated so that they would arrive on scene as the RhAF were making their attack.

Soon the order to launch the operation was received and the Alouettes carrying the forty-five SAS operators were on their way. Meanwhile, at the FAF, the rest of the SAS attack group had already boarded the six Dakotas which were to carry them to Mkushi and were awaiting takeoff.

When it arrived, the initial airstrike on Mkushi was largely unsuccessful, with only two of the participating Canberras dropping their Alpha bombs on target. The accompanying Hunters were more accurate, hitting the main camp and several of its eight satellites hard.

With the Hunters still swooping over the scene to strafe the scattering ZIPRA, the Dakotas made their low-level run in. Soon the SAS were out of the doors in tight sticks. They were jumping so low that reserve parachutes hadn't been issued. In few seconds they had available to observe the camp, they saw a scene of devastation. Smoke and fires were everywhere. Here and there K-cars were prowling and the thud of their 20mm cannons rent the air, cutting in above the noise of aero engines and small arms fire.

As soon as the SAS men hit the ground they began to form up. It quickly transpired that some sticks had landed closer to the camp than was healthy while others dropped quite some distance from the start lines. Some confusion reigned for a short while until the SAS could sort themselves out. There was no way they could hope to encircle Mkushi; instead the only way to deal with those terrorists who hadn't managed to flee would be to sweep through the camp in skirmish lines. Soon, quite a number of ZIPRA began to mistakenly run into the SAS as they sprinted blindly away from the airstrikes. They were quickly dealt with.

About ten miles south of Mkushi, at the staging post where the helicopters were to be refuelled and rearmed, another Dakota was making its run in. Aboard were the team who would be responsible for running and defending the site. At the head of the stick was sixty-six year-old SAS veteran – on TF call up – Regimental Sergeant Major (RSM) Standish. RSM Standish was far too old for active service – or indeed any military service – but it seems that no one dare explain the fact to him. He'd wangled his way onto the operation by sheer force of personality and was determined to make sure the part of the operation which was his responsibility ran like clockwork.

RSM Standish and his men parachuted into the location without incident and immediately set about preparing themselves for what was to come next.

Two Dakotas were following on close behind their own and would be over the staging post in a matter of minutes, they'd be paradropping 55 gallon drums of avgas (aviation fuel) onto the location so that the choppers already on the scene at Mkushi could refuel on their way back to Rhodesia. The Alouettes were only possessed of relatively short range and the flight to Mkushi would have used much of their fuel. It was vital that the staging post be operational before they arrived so they could brim their tanks for the return journey. Canisters containing 20mm ammo were also to be dropped, thus allowing the K-cars to rearm as well as refuel before rejoining the fight.

No sooner had the fuel drums hit the dirt than the first choppers began to make an appearance. Directing his men while helping to roll the heavy barrels out of harm's way, RSM Standish ensured that the Alouettes could be immediately tended to upon landing.

Back at Mkushi, the forty-five strong SAS team who'd been deposited by helicopter were fanning out to their various positions where they hoped to interdict the terrorists as they ran for the safety of the bush. In charge was Captain McKenzie (he of the Cabora Bassa operation). As well as being top heavy with RPD light machineguns, the team had brought an 81mm mortar and plenty of ammunition and were setting the weapon up to provide fire support to the assault groups.

As the assault groups began to move through the chest high grass towards the main camp, all around them the bush was on fire. Exploding bombs had touched off the tinder dry vegetation to create a wall of dense choking smoke which caught in the back of the throat and stung the eyes.

There were contacts happening all around as the panicked terrorists ran into the SAS. Some fought back while others tried to escape, but all were dealt with accordingly.

One SAS NCO was mortally wounded in one of these exchanges before his comrades could suppress the enemy. All the ZIPRA involved were killed in the exchange and it was only when the operators were checking them for intelligence that they realised that one of the bodies was a woman. Like the others, she was dressed in full ZIPRA khaki uniform and carrying a rifle. Without closer inspection she was indistinguishable from the men.

This was a shock to those involved and they passed on the discovery to 'Sunray' (the operational commander). While they were aware that ZIPRA were training female terrorists and this wasn't the first time the SAS had encountered them, they certainly weren't expecting to find themselves fighting women at Mkushi!

Elsewhere along the sweep line, another SAS team encountered a group of ZIPRA. They were all women led by what the SAS later presumed to be an instructor; as the SAS hove into view the terrorists opened fire, seriously injuring one of the operators. A brutal close-quarter's firefight ensued and a medic was called for. As tended to the wounded trooper, he too came under fire – the terrorists weren't signed up to the Geneva Convention, neither did they recognise any informal 'rules' of war.

Undeterred, the medic continued his work and even managed to get the unconscious operator to safety under a hail of bullets.

The SAS dealt with these terrorists exactly the same as they would have had they been men.

As the SAS moved forward, they found themselves on the perimeter of the main camp. They knew that it was surrounded by machinegun posts, bunkers and trench lines but were expecting to find them empty as the terrorists fled for their lives from the air attacks. However, it quickly became apparent that at least some ZIPRA were prepared to stand their ground.

The SAS soon became embroiled in a series of vicious engagements with terrorists who weren't going to allow the Rhodesian's to simply walk into Mkushi. One by one, the positions were cleared with small arms fire, grenades and well aimed RPG-7 rounds. K-cars, flying low overhead were called upon time and time again to bring their 20mm main armament into play against those ZIPRA who were proving particularly stubborn.

Incredibly, the main resistance was being put up by the female ZIPRA, who proved they knew how to use their weapons and were being far more aggressive than their male counterparts. The disparate groups of ZIPRA, both male and female, sought cover wherever they could find it behind trees and rocks, in gulley's and the nearby riverbank. They bided their time until the SAS got within range before opening up, sometimes even managing to stay hidden as the operators passed them. The SAS found themselves being shot at from all sides, including from behind. It was a desperate, confusing fight yet, steadily, the Rhodesian's systematically ground down the terrorist's will to resist.

When they finally broke into the main camp, the carnage wrought by the airstrikes was clear. Bomb craters and bodies were scattered across the area for as far as the eye could see. Overhead, the K-cars were still prowling, their cannons erupting occasionally as they spotted what was left of the enemy.

Large portions of the camp had survived the bombing and thus remained intact. The SAS men were impressed at how orderly it was. Dotted around the parade ground were a plethora of buildings; barracks, stores, an armoury, a medical centre, a large kitchen and dining facilities, there was even a library. The SAS also quickly uncovered an underground bunker. The place was identified as the HQ of the camp commandant though the CO and his staff were nowhere to be found.

It was clear right from the start that the place was under Russian influence, a large Soviet hammer and sickle symbol was daubed on one of the buildings and scattered around in the detritus was further evidence of the Russian connection in the shape of communist handbooks, training manuals, propaganda pamphlets and the like. Someone even found a Soviet General's uniform!

While the SAS were busying themselves searching the camp for items of intelligence which could be transported back to Rhodesia for appraisal by the CIO and SB, one small unit detached itself from the team and set off, in one of the Russian made vans which were lying abandoned around the site, for the main dirt road which connected Mkushi with the outside world.

The Rhodesian planners had presumed that the Zambian authorities would not stand idly by as Rhodesian forces made three large-scale attacks inside their country. As such, an intervention by Zambian air and ground units was not only likely but expected. The SAS were determined to make sure that no one could interfere with the operation at Mkushi while it was ongoing so the task of the team was to lay some anti-tank mines on the road to discourage any Zambian reaction force from getting into a position where the SAS were forced to engage it.

Unlike in Mozambique, where the Rhodesian's had no qualms about FRELIMO hitting their mines, here it was different. Instead of burying the devices in the earth where they couldn't be seen, after the anti-handling mechanisms had been set they were left on the surface to act as a visual deterrent. The team then took up positions a little way down the road to act as early warning in case the Zambian's showed up.

Back at the camp the haul of intelligence was impressive, apart from a large amount of top secret documentation, when searching the communications block (which had survived the airstrike), the SAS also unearthed the camp's signals codebooks and some Russian made equipment which was hitherto unknown to be in service with the terrorists.

As the men were hard at work searching, gathering captured weaponry and other equipment, a Zambian MiG suddenly screamed over their heads. It was fast and low but turned and climbed away sharply after the pass before disappearing into the afternoon sky without attempting an attack. The SAS knew there were two RhAF Hunters patrolling high overhead ready to pounce on any Zambian plane which tried to intervene in the operation by using force against the ground troops. For their part, the Zambian's would have been watching the Hunters on their radar screens and were mindful to do nothing except make this token gesture.

In the command Dakota which was orbiting high over Lake Kariba as it co-ordinated the attacks on Mkushi and CGT-2, a voice message was transmitted on the main ZAF frequency, warning the Zambian's to stay well away from both sites. The message was repeated several times until the Rhodesian's were sure that it had been received and understood.

The Rhodesian's had been closely monitoring Zambian military and police radio traffic in order that they could appraise what reaction the attacks were having on the authorities.

There had never been a Rhodesian incursion on this scale before and it was quickly revealed that the Zambian's were in a state of virtual panic. In response to Rhodesian warnings for their air force not to interfere as the airstrikes on the three terrorist camps were underway, the ZAF grounded all their planes (the one which overflew Mkushi was the only recorded flight of the day).

As for the army, they too appeared to be paralysed into inaction by the sheer audacity and size of the Rhodesian attack.

The civil authorities fared no better. The Zambian police made sure they kept well away from the scenes of the action and it was later reported that a Zambian police detachment who were manning a small post near Mkushi were so terrified by the commotion that they abandoned their position, fled into the bush and were never seen again!

Whenever they mounted over raids into Zambia, the Rhodesian's were always careful to explain via radio broadcasts on the military and police frequencies, that Rhodesia had no quarrel with Zambia, its government or its people. They were there to attack the ZIPRA terror organisation. That message was repeated throughout this most momentous of days, along with a reminder that – if the Zambian's wanted it to stop – they must first denounce ZIPRA and ZAPU and eject them from their country.

Back at Mkushi, by mid-afternoon the SAS had secured the site. Given the nature of the operation and the fact that the security forces wanted it known that it was in direct response to the shooting down of the Rhodesian airliner, the decision was made to fly a small group of journalists in to the camp and allow them to take photographs and film footage of the scene of the battle. The SAS were determined to allow the press the run of Mkushi for as long as they thought it practicable. The resulting film and stills of uniformed bodies, the training and propaganda literature, the weaponry and everything else which proved the camp was in use for terrorist purposes and not the 'refugee' camp for the elderly, infirm and children which ZIPRA claimed it to be.

There was still much to do and the press weren't due to arrive until the following morning, so the SAS set out to sweep the area for ZIPRA stragglers who may have managed to evade the initial assault.

The following morning, the press people arrived courtesy of a couple of Alouettes and set to work recording the events which had taken place within. The camp was still smouldering from the RhAF airstrikes. The air was thick with the smell of smoke and the sick making stench of rapidly decaying bodies which had been exposed to the African sun for many hours. Overhead, vultures were circling in anticipation of the feeding frenzy to come and predators were warily sniffing around the perimeter, drawn in by the smell of dead flesh and the prospect of an easy meal.

While the reporters, photographers and cameramen looked on, the SAS set light to the remaining buildings. All the captured weapons and equipment was piled into a heap on the parade ground then set ablaze. The ammunition, landmines and other recovered ordnance was thrown into the underground bunker were it would be sent sky high by delayed action explosives after the SAS had withdrawn.

The press people were removed from the scene but RhAF did not have the capacity to lift the SAS in one move, which meant the extraction was to be conducted in two waves.

Leaving the smoking ruins of Mkushi behind, the Rhodesian's moved to a location a little way south to a point which had been earmarked as the HLZ. Soon afterwards the choppers arrived to take the first half of the SAS force back to Rhodesia.

As the rest of the men waited for the Alouettes to return, word came through on the ground commander's radio from one of the outlying protection callsigns that a large group of men were approaching their location.

It was soon confirmed that the party was made up of Zambian infantry, with a few policemen and ZIPRA tagging along. In total there were more than one-hundred, they were all heavily armed and moving towards the hidden SAS positions in a skirmish line. A hurried exchange between the ground commander and his 2ic (second in command) resulted in the order to engage being issued. For reasons already explained, the Rhodesian's had to exercise caution before tangling with the Zambian's so political considerations were always at the forefront of any decision. It was entirely possible that, rather than attempting an attack, these Zambian troops had seen the helicopters lifting off and were under the impression that the Rhodesian's had left the scene. However, their course would bring them directly in among the SAS positions and there was no way that could be allowed to happen.

With them in their sights, the SAS watched and waited as the Zambian's closed. Suddenly the contact was initiated and all hell let loose. Shocked, the Zambian's went to ground before returning fire.

The firefight lasted approximately twenty minutes and, after the Zambian's had been driven off there was forty-seven of their number laying dead in front of the SAS positions. During the contact the SAS had managed to capture two men. One was a very scared looking Zambian Corporal and the other an older, sullen man in ZIPRA uniform.

The SAS had little time for formalities, as the helicopters were due to arrive. Both men would be removed to Rhodesia for interrogation. The Zambian was lucky because he'd be repatriated, but for the ZIPRA man, the war was definitely over.

Operation Gatling had been a resounding success. It demonstrated to the Zambian's that their patronage of the ZIPRA terror machine would no longer be tolerated and to the international community that Rhodesia was prepared to do whatever it took to defeat the communist terrorist threat. They made no secret of the fact that the mission was as a direct result of the ZIPRA shooting down of the Rhodesian airliner and warned that – if the terrorists tried anything like that again – they could expect to be hit even harder.

Over at CGT-2 the small number of aircraft and RLI paratroops available to attack the camp meant that many of its ZIPRA inhabitants were able to successfully flee the scene before the commandos could get to grips with them; that said the RLI managed to kill fifty terrorists without loss to themselves and went on to destroy much of the infrastructure of the camp plus a large amount of weaponry and other equipment.

ZIPRA losses at Freedom Camp and Mkushi were truly spectacular. The RhAF airstrike on FC was estimated to have cost the terrorists between 800 and 1,000 killed and another 600 wounded. The camp itself was severely damaged, with many of its most important facilities completely destroyed. Several East German and Cuban military advisors were also killed in the raid.

At Mkushi, the RhAF and SAS assault group had accounted for an estimated 800 ZIPRA dead and an unknown number wounded (most of them crawled off into the bush to die where they could not be found). The main camp and its satellites were flattened and much vital equipment destroyed. Their own losses were one man killed and one wounded. A couple of the K-cars were damaged by ground fire but only lightly.

For ZIPRA it was a very black few days; they lost a large number of terrorists who would have otherwise ended up inside Rhodesia or (in the case of the women) undertaken important support duties.

Unfortunately, Nkomo and his cronies weren't present at the time of the airstrike; unbeknown to the Rhodesian's they'd been alerted to the raid on FC by the British via an MI6 spy working inside COMOPS so kept well clear of the area. Why they didn't order the evacuation of the three camps prior to the launching of Operation Gatling is anyone's guess but – perhaps – they did so on the advice of the British who were keen to protect their source. Had the Rhodesian's hit empty camps, they may well have suspected their own organisation had sprung a leak. That being the case the obvious place to look would have been COMOPS. For Nkomo and the ZAPU/ZIPRA high command, it was better to have continued access to the inner workings of the Rhodesian's own military machine, so they may have looked upon the taking of casualties as acceptable if it maintained this link? (This is only conjecture on the author's part. It's more likely that, when they got wind of the numbers of SAS and RLI involved, they were confident that, forewarned, their own people would be able to fight them off.)

The mysterious ZIPRA man who'd been captured by the SAS at Mkushi soon turned out to be a star prize. When delivered into CIO and Special Branch hands, his identity was quickly revealed. Mountain Gutu was ZIPRAs Logistics Officer and a very senior figure in the terrorist organisation. He'd been trained by the Soviets in Russia and knew a great deal of classified information which, up to that point, the Rhodesian's had no idea of.

Knowing that his membership of ZIPRA and participation in terrorist activities would result in his execution, Gutu was most keen to spare himself the hangman's noose when he was offered the chance to in exchange for information. *(For the reader's information, death by hanging was the standard penalty for those found guilty of acts of terrorism or being members or otherwise supporting ZIPRA or ZANLA. We are, of course, speaking about a time before the rights of the perpetrators were taken into consideration. The basic principle was if you were a terrorist or connected to terror organisations in any way you should expect to be executed if found guilty.)*

Over the period of his interrogation, Gutu furnished the CIO and SB with much vital intelligence about the inner workings of the ZIPRA machine. The picture the Rhodesian's were able to build up as a result of their captive's eagerness to cooperate was astonishing. Not only did Gutu explain how ZIPRA was administered, he provided the names of almost every senior ZIPRA and ZAPU official who was involved in planning, recruitment and training. Both CIO and SB were staggered by the list of names; although some were already known, the vast majority had thus far managed to sail under the Rhodesian intelligence radar. All the names were carefully checked and files were compiled. At some point in the future, these men could probably expect to find themselves in the sights of the SAS or Selous Scouts.

Gutu also reveal the locations of several hitherto unknown ZIPRA camps and within days of his capture RhAF Canberras mounted a successful airstrike on a main ZIPRA supply depot near Lusaka.

Unknown ZIPRA FOBs and holding camps, plus the routes being used to supply them were also part of the haul which Gutu supplied.

To round things off, he told his captors of a secret underground prison which was being used to hold kidnapped black Rhodesian civilians (it was standard practice for the terrorist to coerce people in Rhodesia's Tribal Trust Lands into helping them. They used murder, beatings and rape as weapons but also kidnap. They'd take family members and hold them captive in order to force cooperation among otherwise reluctant locals).

The Selous Scouts were tasked with rescuing these Rhodesian citizens and returning them to safety. In a hostage rescue mission which was worthy of any in Special Forces history, the Scouts stormed the prison, killing the ZIPRA guards, freeing the inmates and choppering them back to Rhodesia.

In return for his cooperation, the Rhodesian authorities made good on their promise and, instead of the scaffold, Gutu was sent to prison. He was kept in isolation where his only visitors were the CIO and SB officers who dropped by occasionally to quiz him about other matters pertaining to ZIPRA.

With all this information and more in their possession, the Rhodesian's knew their forces were going to be very busy over the weeks and months to come.

TEN: THE RAILROAD INCIDENT. 1978

To the casual observer, the SAS' attention appeared to be focused on ZIPRA. In actual fact, and apart from to occasional large-scale camp attack like the one made against Mkushi, the threat from the east remained the most serious cause for concern. ZANLA was considered the more dangerous opponent and, with the continuing overt help from Mozambique's ruling junta, FRELIMO, were threatening to overwhelm the Rhodesian ability to counter them.

In December 1978, Rhodesian intelligence and the BSAP Special Branch found themselves with an early Christmas present. The man in question was part of the ZANLA high command in Tete province and very well placed to provide both the CIO and SB with a wealth of intelligence on terrorist operations in that province of Mozambique. It had been a targeted kidnap, with a Selous Scouts 'snatch squad' taking him and spiriting him across the border into Rhodesia.

When suddenly confronted with the same fate as Mountain Gutu, the man began to spill the beans about everything he knew. The flood of information was staggering and both CIO and SB immediately knew that they were able to equip the security forces with intelligence which they could then use to devastation effect.

One twenty-four carat nugget which the captive handed over was the fact that FRELIMO had given ZANLA the use of one of the hangars at an airfield near Tete town.

The terrorists had busied themselves filling the huge building to the rafters with landmines, explosives, arms and ammunition and other ordnance, turning it into the largest ZANLA arms dump in the province.

When the intelligence report detailing the hanger and its significance to ZANLA operations in north-eastern

Rhodesia landed on the desk of RhAF Director of Operations, Air Marshall Norman Walsh, with an attachment from ComOps stating that its destruction was to be given the utmost priority, he wasted no time in attending to the matter.

Word was sent out Number 1 Squadron to mount an attack on the hanger. Fortunately, earlier aerial reconnaissance of the entire area was available and used to plan the strike. It was to be a daylight mission (RhAF aircraft didn't have the capability to mount precision attacks against specific targets at night). A pair of Hunters would hit the hanger with high explosive rockets and let the stored explosives and ammunition do the rest.

Given the very real threat to RhAF aircraft from FRELIMO AA defences, the operation wasn't going to be easy. The Hunters would have to fly all the way in and out at extremely low altitude if they were to stand any chance of evading FRELIMO SAM missiles which everyone knew Freddie would launch at the first available opportunity.

The hunters took off, flying nap of the earth all the way to the target. Although the FRELIMO radar operators had picked them up as they crossed the border, the frequent changes of course meant they were unable to calculate the destination of the intruders and the altitudes such that they were unable to bring their SAMs to bear.

When they arrived over the airfield, the few FRELIMO AA gunners were caught completely off guard. The First Hunter fired a salvo of rockets at the target hanger but missed. Close on its tail, the second aircraft swooped in for its own pass. These rockets were on target. Suddenly the whole hanger erupted. According to the pilots involved the explosion was on a scale they had never witnessed before, indeed, such was the violence of the blast that the shockwave almost knocked both planes out of the sky.

The Hunters didn't hang around to admire their

handiwork, but instead dropped back down to treetop level for the journey home.

Apparently the explosion was such that it was heard across the border in Rhodesia.

The destruction of the arms dump was complete. Not only had it been obliterated but the surrounding hangers and even the buildings further afield were also destroyed in the blast.

In one fell swoop the RhAF had taken out the terrorist's ability to arm and equip their Rhodesia bound gangs. It was a disastrous day for ZANLA on a scale they had never before witnessed, but things were about to get even worse. With one priority target down there was one more to go.

The Rhodesian's knew that ZIPRA, with the help of FRELIMO, would be desperate to make good the losses suffered by the destruction of their main arms dump and, in order to get their offensive against Rhodesia moving again as quickly as possible they would have move in new supplies to the Tete province as quickly as possible.

A detailed appreciation of how this could be achieved was made by ComOps planners and it quickly became clear that their – ZANLAs – options were severely limited. In order to get the required amount of ammunition, explosives etc to 'feed' their Rhodesia bound terror gangs, it was clear that the only way to do it was by train. There was only one line, which ran from Beira into Tete province, and if that could be severed, ZANLAs hopes of rapidly making good their losses would be dashed.

The job was turned over to the SAS at their new depot at Kabrit, located on the edge of New Sarum International Airport near Salisbury.

It was clear from the start that wrecking the line with explosives, or perhaps even derailing a train in the process would not have the desired long-term effect.

What the SAS needed was a target which FRELIMO would be unable to repair so that the line would be out of action permanently.

The Mecito Bridge was the obvious choice for SAS attention, it carried the line over a gorge and, once gone, there would be no rebuilding it without foreign assistance.

The SAS requested intelligence on the bridge and were furnished with a series of RhAF reconnaissance photos, taken at high altitude and it was with these, and the appraisal of the RhAF photographic interpreters, that they began to formulate a plan of action.

The responsibility for the Bridge's destruction was given to Lieutenant 'Mac' McIntosh (the officer who led the ill-fated recce mission into Mozambique) and he assembled a twenty-strong team to carry out the operation.

Working with the intelligence supplied by the RhAF, Lieutenant McIntosh, the callsign's 2ic and a couple of SAS explosives experts began to put together a demolitions plan.

Demolishing a structure, any structure, but especially one the size of the Mecito Bridge called for very careful planning. It was not a case of sticking some dynamite on it, lighting a fuse then standing back as it goes up in a ball of flames – that's the stuff of Hollywood. The aim was always to use the minimum amount of explosives possible, but using those explosives to best effect. To drop the bridge (or 'jack' it in Rhodesian military parlance) the team had to first understand how it was built. Knowing where the load bearing components were would allow the SAS to target them and cause the bridge to collapse. The explosives most often used were military-grade plastic explosives which produced immense shattering power (although, in this instance the SAS would have to make do with the less powerful TNT simply because of shortage problems). When placed correctly at vital points, the force of the explosions could be directed in to the structure itself, creating shockwaves which could easily tear through steel and concrete, causing catastrophic structural failure and collapse.

Setting the explosives would be a time consuming task, requiring skill and patience. Some hours of hard work would be required to rig it for demolition. In this instance, rather than using slow burning fuses which would detonate the PE after the SAS had left the scene, Lieutenant McIntosh had another idea; the ring-main was to be attached to a command detonation unit and the SAS would lay in wait until the first FRELIMO/ZANLA troop or goods train came steaming down the line from Beira. When it did, he would be waiting to blow the bridge to kingdom come and send the train crashing into the gorge below.

There was no time to waste; the bridge had to be destroyed at the earliest opportunity. The plan was given the green light and Lieutenant McIntosh's team moved to a FAF close to the Mozambique border.

Lieutenant McIntosh and his callsign were parachuted into the area in the dead of night. They deliberately dropped a few miles away from the target bridge as they were aware that FRELIMO may be searching the area for Rhodesian saboteurs. The Dakota had observed all the usual precautions on the way in and carried on after dropping the SAS, zigzagging at low level before dropping a few Alpha bombs on a distant FRELIMO outpost.

The country was close and it was hard going but eventually the callsign found themselves at their destination, a little way away from the bridge. The plan was to establish a firm base then move forward into a position where they could put it under observation. Apart from being able to assess the structure at close quarters and decide the best way of placing the charges, they would also be looking for any sign of enemy activity.

Railway lines are notoriously difficult to protect, unless the defenders can place men within visual range of each other all along its length, any saboteur can wreck the lines and keep doing so with virtual impunity. However, with all that was happening, it was entirely possible that FRELIMO may have cottoned onto the fact that this particular train line was vital to ZANLA and could have taken measures to defend critical points along its length which, unlike the tracks themselves, they realised would be impossible to repair if attacked.

Once the SAS got 'eyes on' the bridge, if they saw it was guarded by a detachment of FRELIMO, their plans to jack it would be scuppered.

Given the size of the Mecito Bridge, it had been calculated that it would take no less that 2200lbs (just a few pounds short of one ton) of explosives to bring it down. Obviously, it was impossible for the SAS men to carry that in so the plan was that, once the recce had established that all was clear, a Dakota would be summoned. Guided in by the SAS on the ground, the crew's job would be to drop the explosives and associated detonation equipment directly beside the bridge where the callsign could easily recover and begin the task of placing it.

The following morning, Lieutenant McIntosh and another man made their way towards the bridge and put it under observation.

The good news was that, during the time they were watching there was no sign of FRELIMO activity; no static guards, no roving patrols. The bad news was that the bridge was much larger than the RhAF photographic interpreters had calculated it to be. It spanned a deep, steep sided gorge at the bottom of which ran a river.

Using the intelligence supplied by the RhAF, the SAS had worked out a plan of attack whereby they would approach the bridge from the underside, using a couple of special ladders to access the girder work before spreading themselves out along it to place the charges.

Back at the firm base, the issue of how to get themselves and the explosives under the bridge was resolved via a group discussion with every man, regardless of rank, having equal input.

As far as they were all concerned, there was no reason for the mission to be scrubbed so, at the next scheduled radio transmission, they would make a request for the Dakota to drop the explosives.

It was well after dark when the drone of the Dakota's twin radial engines drifted through the bush. The SAS men had assembled at the DZ ready to collect and hide the containers in readiness for the next phase of the mission.

As the Dakota passed low overhead the callsign were expecting to see a gaggle of parachutes blossoming in the sky. Instead there was nothing?

Up in the Dakota, in their haste to rid themselves of the cargo, the dispatchers (who, it transpired, were both inexpcricnccd) failed to wait for the final order to drop the containers. As a result the seconds which elapsed between them ejecting the containers and receiving the instruction to do so meant that each one fell far short of the SAS position. As the explosives floated down into the embrace of the bush far out of view, Lieutenant McIntosh – unaware what had happened – was on the radio asking the Dakota crew why they hadn't dropped the containers. When it became clear that the dispatchers had failed to do their job properly the SAS men were less than happy, communicating their displeasure to the Dakota crew in the most 'robust' terms.

Now Lieutenant McIntosh and his men faced the unenviable task of trudging through dense bush in pitch blackness in search of the missing containers. Once found, they would have to lug them all back to where they should have been dropped in the first place.

Much of the night was spent locating the missing explosives and carrying it back to where it could be hidden beside the bridge (remember there was a ton of TNT plus several rolls of detonating cord, etc).

It was almost first light by the time the callsign had completed their task. They were worn out and still angry as they retreated to the firm base. At the next scheduled radio transmission to SAS HQ, a situation report was made; as well as pointing out the mistake of the RhAF dispatchers in no uncertain terms and what that mistake had meant for the callsign, it was communicated that they intended to lay the explosives that coming night.

When darkness fell the team moved up to where they'd hidden the demolitions gear and, after retrieving it, made their way onto the bridge. They knew that no trains ran along the line after dark and so could carry out the task without interruption.

Given the fact that they were forced to improvise a method of getting men and explosives under the bridge, everything about this phase was all a bit Heath-Robinson. Ropes were secured around the metal railings then cast over the side into the ravine below. Lieutenant McIntosh and another man climbed out over the edge of the bridge before abseiling into the abyss. It was now their job to lay the charges and link them all together to produce an instantaneous detonation. It was going to be a hard and dangerous task.

High above the river they'd have to shuffle along narrow girders then up and down gradients as they made their way to the points where the TNT could be placed, spooling out the det cord to form the ring main. One slip or momentary lapse of concentration would see them fall to their deaths.

Up top, apart from a couple of operators who were on guard and covering both approaches, the rest of the callsign were feeding the TNT over the side where the two men could get to it. Each charge was extremely heavy so it had to be presented in just the right place where it could be grabbed and swung into position.

As the night wore on it became clear to all involved that that the task could not be completed in one go. There was no alternative but to do as much as possible before abandoning the job and retiring to the bush before sun up.

Lieutenant McIntosh and his companion eventually tied ropes onto their 'hot extraction' harnesses (a harness worn by SAS operators so they could be winched to safety by helicopter in situations where it was not practicable to make a landing – in other words in close contact with the enemy) and then were hauled up by the others.

The scene was cleared and, when Lieutenant McIntosh was sure no trace of their presence had been left behind, they retired into the scrub. The plan now was to wait here where they could see the bridge.

As the sun rose it became apparent that the charges were on full view. Anyone looking over the side of the bridge could not fail to see them. The SAS had to hope that no FRELIMO came along with orders to check the line and the critical points along it for evidence of sabotage.

The men were all exhausted and, with usual protocols being observed, they took some well-earned rest.

Around mid-afternoon they heard the rattle of a small diesel engine. Immediately the callsign were at the alert and soon spotted a trolley chugging sedately along the line.

As it closed they were able to see its occupants – half a dozen fully armed FRELIMO. The same thought flashed though everyone's mind; had they been compromised?

As the SAS looked on, the trolley rolled to a halt onto

the bridge and two men stepped out. Rifles slung casually over their shoulders, the pair mooched about on the track for what seemed like an age. Anything more than a casual glance over the edge and down at the structure below would result in the explosives and the white lines of det cord being seen. Lieutenant McIntosh had taken the decision not to set the charges so they could be detonated if necessary and now he was regretting that decision. If the charges were seen, the SAS would have no alternative to withdraw.

Eventually the two men climbed back aboard the trolley and it began the next leg of its journey. The SAS watched it disappear before breathing a collective sigh of relief.

So, FRELIMO were indeed patrolling the track, though not paying much attention to their duties.

Given what had just happened it was imperative that the SAS complete the rigging of the bridge. Then, if the explosives were discovered by the next roving FRELIMO patrol, the bridge and whoever was on it could be sent plunging into the gorge.

That night the callsign returned to their duties and toiled hard through the night to make sure the task was complete. Scrambling around the girders like a latter-day New York skyscraper steel erector, Lieutenant McIntosh double checked everything before finally connecting the ring main to the radio controlled detonation device (which itself had been triple checked prior to connection).

As the new day dawned, the SAS were back in position at their LUP. Everything was now set. As far as Lieutenant McIntosh was concerned, it was pointless targeting the first train which came along; he wanted something which would cause maximum loss to either FRELIMO or ZANLA. Radio reports had told him that a train was being loaded with fresh supplies of ordnance to make up some of the losses suffered when the main

ZANLA arms dump was destroyed but it was still in Beira. A few diesel and steam engines had passed along the line but he stayed his hand on each occasion.

An order, passed during the next scheduled radio transmission, told Lieutenant McIntosh that he wasn't to wait around. ComOps were getting nervous that FRELIMO were sniffing round the area and didn't want the SAS men to find themselves compromised. Therefore the next train which appeared would be the one they'd drop the bridge for.

There appeared to be no fixed schedule in operation for this particular line. The only thing the waiting SAS were sure of was that no trains ran after dark.

The callsign waited and waited then waited some more until – after dark – they heard the unmistakable approach of a steam locomotive. The train was heading north into Tete and would pass the hidden SAS team before it got to the bridge. Lieutenant McIntosh stood everyone to then readied himself with the exploder.

The train was puffing along at about forty miles an hour and the waiting SAS men could see it was hauling quite a number of open goods and passenger carriages. For whatever reason, the goods trucks were at the head of the train – good news for the callsign as they weren't sure who was aboard; unlike the terrorists, the SAS had no desire to include civilians in their actions.

As the train was about to steam onto the bridge Lieutenant McIntosh pressed the button. There was a sudden barrage of explosions, so close together that they almost merged into one as the chain-linked charges went off. There was no time for the train driver to react and the SAS men looked on as the engine and the goods cars disappeared over the edge of the gorge. The shrieks of tortured metal rent the night air as the girder work and the locomotive went crashing into the river.

There were so many goods cars that not all of them had gone the way of the engine which meant the passenger cars at the back, while derailed, remained upright.

The lights in the now stationary passenger cars had suddenly gone off as the power from the locomotive was cut.

Staying in cover, the SAS team looked on as bewildered looking civilians climbed out onto the track and away from the scene of the crash.

Suddenly, a group of uniformed men armed with assault rifles burst from one of the cars, prompting the SAS to open fire. There was a brief but heavy exchange of gunfire before the panicked FRELIMO ran off into the bush.

Leaving their positions, the SAS swept forward towards the wrecked train. A huge pall of steam was issuing from the gorge as the locomotive's boiler emptied itself into the night sky. Weird clanks, metallic creaks, hisses and groans were also emanating from the hole where the bridge had been as the locomotive went through its death throes.

With some men providing cover, a few callsign members boarded the train and quickly searched the compartments. They found a few dazed civilian still aboard but shooed them off and along the track in the direction the train had come.

The passenger cars and guards' van cleared, some of the team set to work placing charges on the wheels and axles of those cars which had not toppled over the edge. The object was simple; to deny FRELIMO the opportunity of recovering the cars and putting them back into service.

Meanwhile a couple of men travelled a few hundred yards down the line and placed an anti-tank mine under one of the rails. The reasoning being that when FRELIMO arrived to access the situation and perhaps carry out a follow up of the saboteurs, the train they came in would detonate the mine and cause the locomotive to derail, causing even more disruption and – possibly –

injuries among the FRELIMO who were aboard.

Ideally, the SAS would have liked to stick around and wait for the recovery train to arrive to clear the track then attack it with RPG-7 rockets and small arms fire but, unfortunately, that was out of the question.

It was now time for Lieutenant McIntosh and his team to go. They'd radioed the codeword which signified 'mission successful' then set off into the darkness of the bush towards the rendezvous with the helicopters.

The Mecito Bridge stayed out of commission for the duration of the war and beyond. As the Rhodesian's predicted, FRELIMO did not have the capacity to rebuild it. They didn't even make any attempt to recover the wrecked cars which were scattered across the track. As far as Freddie was concerned the bridge, this section of track and the rolling stock were now out of commission permanently.

The severing of the one and only means of moving the necessary amount of equipment forward to ZANLA caused the terrorists much grief. They were now forced to rely on convoys of trucks which themselves were highly vulnerable to Rhodesian laid mines and ambush teams. The process was slow and ZANLA efforts to put terror gangs across the border were severely impacted as a result.

As for the SAS' parting shot, the landmine laid on the track, FRELIMO did indeed send a train packed with troops to the scene but the SAS men who laid the device were spotted by one of the train passengers who was lurking unseen in the bush. He reported the incident to FRELIMO and they were able to avoid it.

So, 1978 went out with a literal bang for the Rhodesian Special Air Service. They'd mounted some of the most ambitious operations of the war to date. However 1979 was to see even more daring operations into Zambia,

Mozambique and even Botswana.

The End (or is it?)
Please see the next page

If you would like to read about the SAS in 1979 including the operation to assassinate Joshua Nkomo, the daring daylight raid into Lusaka to attack and destroy ZIPRAs intelligence service headquarters, the spectacular attack on the main fuel storage depot in Beira and the audacious beyond top-secret mission to wrest control of the country from Robert Mugabe then please see my other book 'The Rhodesian SAS: Their Most Daring Missions' which is available in various formats on Amazon or from selected booksellers.

Over the next few pages I'd also like to introduce you to some of my other books which should be of interest. (For a complete list please visit Amazon and search for 'Bravo Ten' by Andy Ryan)

Thanks for reading and please keep on reading for the next few pages.

Andy Ryan.

BRAVO TEN

Rhodesia was one of the very last colonial outposts in southern Africa. She had long served Great Britain well, in both peace and war. During World War II, many Rhodesians rallied to the mother counties aid, serving in all branches of His Majesties armed forces, including the fledgling SAS. Her last major act of solidarity with the UK was during the Malayan emergency of 1951 to 1953.

Fighting a guerrilla war for which it was ill prepared, the British Army soon realised the need for a Special Forces unit. The Special Air Service Regiment was duly resurrected and organised into four operational Squadrons. A, B and D Squadrons were drawn from the British Army, while C Squadron was raised from Rhodesian volunteers. When the Malayan conflict came to an end the British gave the SAS a permanent place in its order of battle, but C Squadron quietly disbanded and its members returned home to civilian life in Rhodesia. In 1961, the Rhodesian government decided to reform C Squadron as a counter to the increasing threat of communist insurgency within her borders......

The decision to reinstate C Squadron proved prudent for, after Rhodesia finally made a unilateral declaration of independence on November 11th 1965 and broke away from UK rule, both the Russian and Chinese backed communist terrorist movements known to the world as ZIPRA and ZANLA saw their chance to move in for the kill. Standing alone, hamstrung by international sanctions and facing vastly numerically superior enemy forces, Rhodesia astounded the world by not only holding the enemy off, but taking the fight to them in their host countries of Zambia and Mozambique, killing countless thousands of terrorists in the process.

In 1976 FRELIMO, the ruling party of Mozambique, declared war on Rhodesia and brought her sizeable and well equipped army into the fray alongside their ally,

Robert Mugabe's ZANLA. Despite this, the Rhodesian security forces refused to yield. Indeed, they responded by upping the terrorist body count even further.

By 1978 the war had intensified to the degree that the drain on Rhodesia's limited white manpower was beginning to tell. Conscription was widened and C Squadron was expanded and given Regimental Status. In June of that year it became the 1st SAS Regiment with three operational Squadrons (A, B and C). Its tasking was simple, find and destroy the enemy and its leaders and smash their ability to wage war.......

A Few of the many reviews of Bravo Ten:

I bought this book to read on a flight to Australia. I couldn't put it down. I was supposed to be seeing the sights and all I could do is read this book.

I couldn't put this book down. The stories contained in these pages are jaw dropping and had my pulse pounding. I found myself burning with anger at how Mugabe and Nkomo were allowed to destroy such a wonderful country while the world turned a blind eye.

Great telling of how things were in the day...

The Rhodesian SAS: Their Greatest Missions

From the Author of 'BRAVO TEN', the explosive true story of some of the greatest secret operations of the Rhodesian SAS....

At the height of the cold war, the small landlocked country of Rhodesia found herself ranged against two powerful communist terrorist armies who, in turn, were backed by Soviet Russia and China. The strategic aim of both backers was the installation of a regime friendly to their respective brands of communism and in so doing create a vital regional presence upon which they could then expand. For the terrorist organisations of ZIPRA and ZANLA, they had but one objective; to take control of one of the continent's most prosperous nations.

By 1979 the Rhodesian bush war had been raging for over fifteen years. What had started with the murder of a white man by black nationalists in 1964 was to turn into the bloodiest war ever to have been witnessed in southern Africa.

This book focuses on the final year of the war, when the fighting was at its most intense.

The need for Special Forces to take the fight to the terrorists had never been greater. Fortunately for the Rhodesian's, their military possessed a secret weapon which proved devastating in combat and the scourge of terrorists in Zambia, Mozambique and beyond; their very own Special Air Service Regiment.

Operating deep in the unforgiving African bush; deploying by vehicle, helicopter or parachute, often isolated from help and facing overwhelming odds, the Rhodesian SAS Ranged far behind enemy lines to strike at the very heart of the enemy, wreaking untold damage to the terrorist machines of ZIPRA and ZANLA.

Time after time the SAS regiment demonstrated to the world that the Rhodesian army possessed a Special Forces unit whose abilities were second to none.

The author presents the little known story of a truly elite band of Special Forces soldiers and places the reader at the very heart of some of their most daring missions. Join the Rhodesian SAS deep behind enemy lines and learn the secrets of 'those who dared'.

Combat and Survival Secrets of the Rhodesian SAS

The Rhodesian SAS was a highly secretive and specialised unit which carried out some of the most spectacular Special Forces missions of the 1970s. Their reputation was second to none and their abilities the envy of similar units the world over.

Now, Andy Ryan, author of 'Bravo Ten' and 'The Rhodesian SAS: Their Most Daring Missions' lifts the lid on the operational techniques of these elite troops.

Sections include personal preparation, insertion & extraction, evasion, survival and much more.

It's a must read for anyone with an interest in the Rhodesian SAS, the bush war and Special Forces in general.

The Raid on St. Nazaire

During WW2, St. Nazaire was the most strategically important naval facility in the whole of occupied Europe. It was vital to the Nazi war effort because it was the only place outside Germany where the mighty Tirpitz battleship could be repaired and refitted. Having such a base meant that this most powerful of warships could be unleashed into the North Atlantic to attack the vulnerable allied supply lines and win the war for the Nazis.

Central to the drama was the enormous 'Normandie' dry dock. If the Germans could make use of the dock to repair and refit Tirpitz, then the whole balance of the war would be tipped in their favour. The Germans knew this and the British knew it too. The British Prime Minister,

Winston Churchill, was determined that the Normandie
dock be put out of commission.

The plan was audacious and desperate in equal
measure. No-one believed it could possibly work, yet the
situation was so critical that it was put into effect....

On the night of 28th of March 1942 a small flotilla of
mostly wooden boats sailed into the heavily defended
Loire estuary to begin what was to become known as 'the
greatest raid of all'.........

Kill Pablo Escobar

During the 1980's a brutal war had raged between the
two leading Columbian crime cartels for control of the
cocaine trade into the USA. It was a conflict which saw
countless deaths and showed no sign of ending. To break
the stalemate, the Cali Cartel knew they would have to
smash the Rival Medellin Cartel once and for all, and the
only way to do that would be to kill its leader, the
notorious Pablo Escobar.

In complete secrecy a team of mercenaries led by an ex
Rhodesian SAS operator were assembled. If they brought
the Cali Cartel bosses Escobar's head they would be
given $1,000,000.

Thus was set in motion a daring operation to attack
Escobar's fortress hideout, the Hacienda Napoles, and
assassinate the Medellin Cartel's godfather.

Andy Ryan, author of Bravo Ten, brings this explosive
true story to life, taking the reader by the scruff of the
neck and planting them in the epicentre of the action. It's
a tale of intrigue, daring, and endurance which will have
you on the edge of your seat.

Dare you join the team as they attempt to kill Pablo

Escobar?

Please remember: These and more titles by Andy Ryan are available in all formats via Amazon, while some can also be purchased through selected booksellers.

www.ingramcontent.com/pod-product-compliance
Lightning Source LLC
Chambersburg PA
CBHW071948150726
47999CB00001B/352